Forty Modern Catalan Poems

HOMAGE TO JOAN GILI
ON HIS EIGHTIETH BIRTHDAY

Forty Modern Catalan Poems
Chosen and Introduced by
ARTHUR TERRY
with English Prose Translations by
Members of The Anglo-Catalan Society

1987
THE ANGLO-CATALAN SOCIETY

THE ANGLO-CATALAN SOCIETY
OCCASIONAL PUBLICATIONS

© *The Anglo-Catalan Society*

Produced and Typeset by Sheffield Academic Press
Printed by Dotesios (Printers) Limited
Cover design by Joan Gili

ISSN No. 0144-5863
ISBN No. 0 9507137 3 2

CONTENTS

Era tan trist l'amor a l'ombrosa vora enllacada
  dels records adormits, tan solitari en la nit
dels rossinyols—ah dolcíssima cosa certa, certa,
  cant absolut, per damunt l'alba que et trenca—era tan
pàl·lid dins la profunda rodona dels tells—cristal·lina
  de primavera, però sols en l'altura—que el mar
ens ha obsedit, perquè fos l'estrella més pura, si hi era,
  i ens acuités el Temps, i el pensament, exaltat
sobre l'escuma errabunda, engendrés ocells sense nombre
  que el seguissin, oh blancs, gais cavallers del seu vent!
Fins que ens ha pres una illa més verda enllà de les illes,
  verda com si tot el que dins terra és impuls
dolç i obstinat de pujar per ser llum amb la llum contra
                                        [l'ombra
  triomfés allí ona per ona, en l'espai
indecís—i en els ulls i en l'ànima: oh més intensa
  suavitat abans d'un occident més secret;
oh cant líric que es dreça a l'extrem abrupte del somni,
  veu i món acabant junts sobre el buit inhumà!

Love was so sad on the dark, muddy bank of sleeping memories, so lonely in
the night of the nightingales—o sweetest of things, certain, certain, absolute
song, above the dawn which breaks you—it was so pale in the deep circle of
lime-trees—translucent with spring, though only high up—that the sea
obsessed us: that the star, if it were there, might be more pure, and time
might spur us on, and thought, soaring above the wandering foam, might
give birth to countless birds, which would follow it, gay riders of its wind!
Until we were taken by a greener isle beyond the islands, green as if all that
within the earth is a gentle and stubborn impulse to become light with the
light against darkness triumphed there, wave upon wave, in uncertain
space—and in the eyes and the soul: o intensest gentleness before a more
secret west; o lyric song which rises at the sheer edge of sleep, voice and
world ending together above the inhuman void!

Torna a tenir-me el vell parc; al llarg dels meus versos les
                                            [aigües
    llisquen monòtonament com un destí presoner.
Ja no el recordo de vist, sinó de com el preveia,
    canvi més ric i més pur de l'alegria del mar,
l'últim flotó maragdí del rumb nocturn. Però encara
    més innocentment tantes imatges i tant
ai! d'impensable sentit se m'han canviat i es contenen
    en el fervor dels dos enamorats juvenils
que al bell cor de la immensa ciutat fumosa ens obriren
    llur paradís ple de llum, de voluptat i de risc.
I m'és dolç de comprendre que, dels feliços, agraden
    únicament als déus els que han volgut, com els déus,
sota el llit amorós l'onada inestable i, bevent-los
    les rialles, els vents que han mesurat el gran freu.

(*Elegies de Bierville*, III)

CARLES RIBA

The ancient park receives me again; along my verses the waters glide monotonously like an imprisoned fate. I remember, not from sight, but from the way I foresaw it, a richer, purer transmutation of the sea's happiness, the final emerald cluster of the nocturnal course. But still more innocently so many images and so much, alas, unthinkable meaning have changed for me and are contained in the passion of the young lovers who, right in the heart of the vast smoky city, unlocked for us their paradise full of light, pleasure and risk. And it is sweet to me to realize that, of the happy ones, they alone please the gods who, like the gods, have desired beneath their bed of love the restless waves and, drinking their laughter, the winds which have measured the great channel.

JOAN GILI

Joan Gili is a fine example of the true Anglo-Catalan. Since his arrival in this country he has experienced to the full the pleasures and the pains that attend the most difficult condition, genuine dual nationality. Over the past fifty-four years he has acquired the culture, the tastes, the humour, the language, the manner of an Englishman. But this has been no mere exchange of old for new, for in the process he has lost nothing of his Catalan identity and personality. His affection for England and his understanding of all that Britain means has not in the least replaced his love of his homeland and the Catalan people, whose values and aspirations are as much part of his everyday life in his Oxfordshire home as they could be if he lived anywhere in the *Països Catalans*. His remarkable command of English has not come at the expense of the slightest diminution of his linguistic feeling and skill in his native tongue; and he is as familiar with current ideas and events, for example in art and literature, in his native Barcelona as in London. Joan reacts to life with the warmth, the spontaneity and the earnest concern of Mediterranean man while tempering all with the practicality, the objectivity, the moderation of the man of the North.

Books have always been in Joan Gili's blood—grandson of one publisher, son of another, nephew of another (Joan, Lluís and Gustau)—and indeed it was his youthful passion for English literature that first brought him to these shores. Joan's particular interest at that time was the English short story and his correspondence with Henry C. Warren on the subject led to his first visit to London in 1933. Soon afterwards he took the momentous decision to make his life in England. There followed acquaintance and friendship with figures such as Stephen Spender, Hermon Ould, Kingsley Martin, V.S. Pritchett, Alan Rawsthorne, Richard Church, Harry Blech, etc. But Joan's line to Barcelona was never severed, for back down it there flowed articles and commentaries on English literature which were published by his friend, later his brother-in-law, J.V. Foix in *La Publicitat*. There were also regular 'letters from England' and occasional translations into Catalan of pages from D.H. Lawrence, Katherine Mansfield, T.S. Eliot and other modern writers.

But Joan also had an eye for business, and in April 1935 he opened the Dolphin Bookshop in Cecil Court, off Charing Cross Road, London, specializing in Spanish and Catalan books. This venture not only filled a notable gap in the British book trade but it took Joan into a long and successful career as this country's leading Hispanic bookseller. His marriage in 1938 to his charming British wife, Elizabeth, sealed a romance which nearly fifty years on still remains idyllic. Elizabeth, too, has become truly Anglo-Catalan, partnering Joan in all his business and literary enterprises as well as running an international household and raising an Anglo-Catalan family of two sons and a daughter.

The Spanish Civil War and its aftermath affected Joan deeply. Although he lived the war at a distance, it proved traumatic for him and he readily felt a sense of unity and solidarity with the Catalan exiles from Franco's Spain who came to live in Britain—Trueta, Pi-Sunyer, Batista i Roca, Gerhard, Manyé, Vilanova, etc. From that time on Joan has had a place at the centre of the Catalan cultural scene in Great Britain, acting, for example, as Secretary of the *Jocs Florals de la Llengua Catalana* in exile held in London in 1947, with Elizabeth as the *Reina de la Festa*. With good reason Carles Riba, who dedicated one of his *Elegies* to Joan and Elizabeth, dubbed him Catalan 'Cònsul Cultural a Anglaterra'! And years later, in 1983, President Pujol rewarded his services to Catalonia by decorating him with the *Creu de Sant Jordi*. Joan was, of course, a leading member of that small group of English and Catalan friends who in 1954 founded the Anglo-Catalan Society, the purpose of which was—and continues to be—to promote knowledge of Catalonia and Catalan culture in Great Britain and elsewhere. Joan and Elizabeth have been fervent and loyal members, and Joan has served regularly on the Committee and as President for a four-year term. In 1979 he was elected life President d'Honor of the Society in succession to J.-M. Batista i Roca. For nearly half a century Joan and Elizabeth have given generously of their time, their expertise, their hospitality and their resources to help scholars, students and indeed anyone interested in the history and culture of Catalonia and Spain. In 1970 the Association of Hispanists of Great Britain and Ireland made Joan an honorary member of their Association; and in 1986, following the visit of King Juan Carlos I to Oxford, Joan was made by him a *Comendador de la Orden de Isabel la Católica*.

The fullness of Joan's early literary ambition was frustrated by the events of 1936 to 1945, but his talent soon revealed itself strongly in the traditional way of his family. The Dolphin Book Company, transferred from London and established in Oxford in 1940, had by now become not only a bookseller but also a small publishing house specializing in producing high quality editions of works of Hispanic interest. Joan himself has directed all the publications, designing the books physically and advising the authors on the presentation of their manuscripts. (The series in which this homage appears was brought into the world with him in close attendance and he has been its mentor ever since.) Some of Joan's own work, too, has been published by Dolphin. His *Catalan Grammar* (1943), now in its 4th edition, is a standard work for English-speaking learners of Catalan throughout the world. But there have also been his most accomplished translations of Carles Riba's *Poems* (1964), his *Forms and Words* (1980) (translations of a collection of poems by Espriu), and his editions of two 15th-century Catalan manuscripts, found by Joan himself, *Lapidari* (1977) and *Lo cavall* (1985); for, beginning with the purchase of Foulché-Delbosc's library in 1939, Joan has also become one of the leading specialists in Hispanic antiquarian books and manuscripts. His own collection, containing rarities such as *Els usatges de Barcelona* of 1490 and the 1507 edition of the *Llibre del Consolat de Mar*, is perhaps the most important one of its kind in private hands. It is to Joan Gili that collectors all over the world turn for specialist and rare items; to their chagrin they may find that not everything he has is for sale!

The art of the translator has always been close to Joan's heart. Since his youthful apprenticeship with Josep M. Llovera in the 1920s Joan has become a master—see for example his inspired translations of Lorca (F.G.L., *Poems*, [with Stephen Spender] Dolphin, 1939, and the Penguin *Lorca*, first publ. in 1960) as well as those Catalan works mentioned above; it is a discipline in which he excels and takes great interest. This, together with his love of poetry, has made an anthology of Catalan poems with English translations a fitting and an obvious way for the Anglo-Catalan Society to commemorate his 80th birthday and show its affection and regard for him. It is a small token of the Society's appreciation and gratitude to its President d'Honor for all he has done for its members both corporately and as individuals; and it is a way of congratulating him and wishing him many more years of health (at 80 he still, scandalously, plays a strong game of tennis) and happiness with his delightful Elizabeth at his side, in the land he has made his own.

GEOFFREY J. WALKER

PREFACE

When I was asked to compile a short anthology of modern Catalan poetry for the present occasion, it struck me that this would be a good opportunity to put together a number of poems which I personally admired and which might also, I hoped, appeal to the friend whose continuing presence and example I and my fellow-members of the Anglo-Catalan Society were eager to celebrate. The result is something in the nature of a sampler of modern Catalan poetry from, roughly, 1939 to the present: in no sense a comprehensive selection, but at least an attempt to suggest the range, and as far as possible, the quality, of the best work published in the last forty years or so. Again, rather than concentrate on half-a-dozen major figures, I thought it would be more interesting to include as many poets as space allowed, irrespective of age or reputation, and to represent each of them, with one exception, by a single poem. This, to be sure, does less than justice to those poets, like Riba and Espriu, whose finest poems are often part of a longer sequence, or to a poet like Agustí Bartra, whose imagination seems to work most naturally in the large-scale poem; on the other hand, it has the effect of directing one's attention to the poems themselves, rather than their authors—no bad thing, perhaps, at a time when the arts in general, like so much else, have to contend increasingly with the cult of 'personalities'.

The wish to concentrate on individual poems also led me to avoid any chronological ordering, whether by poems or poets. Instead, as I sifted through the poems I had already chosen, a certain sequence seemed to emerge, with little need for manipulation on my own part. This sequence should become clear to anyone who reads through the anthology from beginning to end, though at times the connections are more intuitive than strictly arguable, and there is nothing definitive about my arrangement. The latter is partly thematic, though not, I hope, too predictably so; as a rule, differences in handling a common theme are more revealing than similarities, and sharp juxtapositions tend to point up the qualities of individual poems more effectively than smooth transitions. In the end, however, what binds these poems together is not so much their subject-matter as the feeling for a particular language, with all the cultural resonances that implies, and the way they use that language to explore many different kinds of experience, both private and collective.

It is, of course, dangerous to generalize on the basis of a small selection of poems; nevertheless, if there is one generalization worth risking, it would be something along the lines I have just hinted at: the fact that, in many of the poems I have chosen, there is a constant interplay between the personal and the public, a sense that neither should be allowed to exclude the other, still less that the course of public events should be felt to compromise the integrity of the individual.

These difficult claims, and the tensions they imply, are nowhere more evident than in the poems composed during, or shortly after, the Civil War by older writers like Carles Riba, Josep Carner and J.V. Foix. The third of Riba's *Elegies de Bierville*, written in exile in France early in 1939, is a case in point: though it owes its special place in the anthology to the fact that it is dedicated to the Gilis— could it really date from almost half a century ago?—the complex synthesis which it offers brings together a number of strands, each of which is crucial to Riba's development as a poet. One of these is his Hellenism: not only his use of classical myths as a means of structuring his own experience, but also his choice of a verse-line based on the Greek hexameter. Another, more closely connected with circumstances, is his sense of exile as a *despullament* or stripping down to essentials, a time of personal privation which can be made to stand for the collective experience. Thus in the context of the rest of the sequence, the actual itinerary described in the poem— a journey to London and Belfast and the subsequent return to France—comes to seem part of a larger pattern, a design which hints, however obscurely, at the possibility of renewal. Yet what is most impressive, at least in the original, is something else: the way in which Riba allows the concentrated, Symbolist language of his earlier poems to expand to take in the mood of restlessness and exaltation which leads to the final immage of the young lovers

This closing paradox—the sense that what is most precious in life depends on a conscious acceptance of 'risk'—continues to reverberate through much of Riba's later poetry. For Foix, on the other hand, the notion of instability is not so much a product of circumstances as part of reality itself, of a world in which the limits between the 'real' and the 'unreal' are constantly blurred. In many of his poems, like the one included here, everything, not excepting the personality of the poet himself, is subjected to a continual process of metamorphosis. Yet, though he often comes close to Surrealism, especially in his use of dream material, Foix always remains in control of his poems: for all the changing appearances, the emotions these evoke are direct and powerful, and the original situation, however transformed, loses none of its force. Again, as in the very different case of Riba, one has the sense of an established poet attempting to confront the general catastrophe without compromising the nature of his own imagination. So here, the anecdote of a wartime parting is transformed into a private myth which in turn suggests the deeper processes which for Foix determine the whole of human existence.

It is a measure of Foix's skill that he can move with apparent ease from the dimension of cosmic myth to the simple poignancy of 'els passaports són vells i sangosos els cors' ('the passports are out of date and hearts are bleeding') or to the historical perspectives opened up by the slight archaism in the last line: 'Onegen *foramur* banderes esquinçades' ('Torn flags wave outside the walls'). This last image also occurs, with great dignity, in the late sonnet by Josep Carner, the great master of the generation of Riba and Foix. What strikes one, however, in this and other poems concerned with war and its aftermath, is not so much the elegiac note as the way this combines with other moods—despair, contempt, qualified hope—to suggest something like the full spectrum of possible experience. Again, one comes back to Riba's image of 'stripping-down', to the way in which the pressure of circumstances leads not only to protest, but to the kind of intense self-scrutiny which is the necessary preliminary to renewal. In the poetry of Salvador Espriu, for example, the attempt at introspection is carried out with the pessimism, and at times the self-accusing vehemence, of the Old Testament prophets. Thus in *Llibre de Sinera* ('Book of Sinera')—'Sinera' is Arenys (de Mar), the

poet's birthplace, spelt backwards—the 'itinerary' on which the
sequence is based is more metaphysical than real: though life has
returned to Sinera after the devastations of war, this life still has its
sinister aspects, and the poet's own 'return' is seen as the final stage
in his journey to death. Though the emphasis is on guilt and personal
failure, the concluding epigraph from II *Corinthians*, 7—'With you I
die and with you I live'—suggests, like much of the sequence itself,
that the speaker's own expiation takes its value from the collective
context. If, as he says at one point, 'He donat la meva vida pel difícil
guany /d'unes poques paraules despullades' ('I have given my life for
the difficult gain of a few naked words') the cost of the acquisition,
and the modesty of the claim, guarantee the integrity of the self-
knowledge which, however minimal, can now be passed on. In the
poem I have chosen, which comes near the end of the sequence, the
inner journey this has entailed is expressed through the difficult
image of the 'wells'—a gradual descent into nothingness where each
step represents a word in a new and necessary language. These are
the 'few naked words' with which the poet has now returned, not in
the expectation of fame—the 'statue' is only a momentary
condensation of human dust—but with the knowledge of his
imminent descent into the anonymity of the dead.

This bleak vision, though not without its moments of genuine
warmth, compels one's admiration, if only for the immense seriousness
with which it re-enacts the traditional concept of poet as spokesman.
What is certain is that the Civil War and the experience of defeat
continue to cast their shadow over even the most recent Catalan
poetry, often at unexpected moments. Thus in Gabriel Ferrater's
'Temps Enrera' ('Time Was') —a poem I shall return to later—the
personal relationship is overshadowed by the spectre of armed
violence, and in the work of a much younger poet, Xavier Bru de
Sala, the spectacle of man's capacity for self-destruction is set in the
context of vanished civilizations.

Such long perspectives tempt one to dwell on the relationship
between modern Catalan poets and earlier poetry in their own
language. Bru de Sala's own poem, for instance, is written in the
characteristic metre—a descasyllabic line, with a caesura after the
fourth syllable—of the great fifteenth-century poet Ausiàs March

(1397-1459), a fact which most Catalan readers could be expected to recognize. This, it seems to me, contributes to both the gravity and the general timelessness of the poem: an echo chamber, to use Feliu Formosa's image, in which both classical and modern allusions can resonate. This, moreover, is not the only poem in the anthology to be written under the sign of Ausiàs March; in each case, what is being invoked is the kind of quality so admirably defined in the sonnet by Francesc Vallverdú: a standard of emotional honesty which never sacrifices harsh truths for poetic effect. It is this, surely, which accounts for the un-selfpitying tone of Rosa Leveroni's moving reflections on love and death, just as it determines the whole thrust of Carles Riba's fine sequence of sonnets, *Salvatge Cor* ('Savage Heart'), whose title itself is adapted from March.

Here, the more speculative movement of the *Elegies* gives way to a dramatic questioning of the possibilities of religious, and more specifically Christian, belief. From the beginning, Riba is concerned with the origins of experience and the extent to which this may be determined by a transcendental power. Again, as in the *Elegies*, the twin theme of memory and oblivion, symbolized by the sleep of Ulysses as he journeys back to Ithaca, plays a cruical part in the process of spiritual rebirth. In the poem included here, which comes shortly before the end of the sequence, Riba uses another traditional theme—the song of Orpheus—to suggest the prime impulse which comes, not from the intellect, but from emotional experience. With this recognition, in turn, comes the sense of identity with the world, and the power—the sense of the absolute—which comes from this. Again—and here one is made to feel the full force of the title—the intellect has no part in this process: the speaker hands himself over to the 'mad acts' which have made him what he is. And the final implication is clear: it is from these, if from anything, that his salvation—the 'great suit' of the closing lines—will come, and it is these actions which encompass love.

Intellect here is not so much denied—the lyrical imagination, of which Riba writes elsewhere, cannot afford to neglect any of the powers at its disposal—as transcended in the interests of a greater synthesis. As Riba implies, the tensions involved in this process can only be lived out in the individual existence, through the specific

occasions which his own poetry can only hint at. Thus it comes as a
pleasant shock to realize that the relationship so beautifully evoked
by Riba's widow, Clementina Arderiu, nine years after his death, is
the very one which lies at the heart of his own, more ambitious work.
The feeling expressed in her modest and courageous poem is 'loving'
in an immediately recognizable sense, one which can only confirm
the truthfulness of Riba's more difficult concept of 'love'.

The concern for truthfulness in personal relations appears in a
number of the poems I have included, more often than not as part of
a wider social context. Here again, one notes what I have called the
interplay between the personal and the public, the attempt, common
to much of the best recent Catalan poetry, to suggest the inter-
dependence of what is essential and what is actual. The kind of
moral stance this can involve is indicated very clearly in a statement
made by Gabriel Ferrater in 1960:

> I take poetry to be a step by step description of the moral life of an
> ordinary man like myself... When I write a poem, the only thing
> which conerns me and gives me trouble is to define as clearly as
> possible my moral standpoint, that is to say, the distance which
> separates the feeling the poem expresses from what one might call
> the centre of my imagination.

Ferrater's own poems, like the one I have included, are often more
subtle than this statement suggests: in their reaction against a too
narrowly conceived 'social realism', they not only give full weight to
personal experience, but show how such experience is constantly
reshaped in the mind, and how this process adds up to the sense of an
individual life. So, in 'Temps Enrera' ('Time Was'), an episode in the
past is re-created as if it were happening in the present. The
sharpness of the opening description, though superficially 'realistic',
already contains hints of the emotional crisis which is to come; in the
central part of the poem, however, the language becomes increasingly
metaphorical, as if to suggest the irrational nature of the lovers' fear.
The main emphasis of the poem—beautifully conveyed in the final
image of alternating warmth and cold—falls on the narrowness of the
line which separates fear from happiness. More subtly, however, it is
the public fear—the threat of military violence—which absolves the
lovers from their private fears—the possible breakdown of their own

relationship—and enables them to overcome what now seems only a momentary lapse.

This kind of honesty in the analysis of personal relationships which is prepared to acknowledge the limits of rationality is also evident in the group of poems about marriage. Though between them they cover a surprisingly wide range of attitudes, they all, it seems to me, avoid very successfully the twin pitfalls of self-indulgence and excessive solemnity. Thus the unpretentious thanksgiving of Miquel Àngel Riera's poem about the extent to which even the most permanent of relationships may rest on coincidence complements Josep Llompart's fine, and quite unsatirical, attempt to suggest the depth of feeling which can underlie even the most apparently routine of marriages. Not that satire is completely absent from such poems: if Noah, in the wonderfully funny poem by Pere Quart, is made to speak in the accents of a Catalan Alf Garnett, this is not only a demonstration of one poet's extraordinary ear for popular speech, but also a reminder of one of the strongest veins in Catalan poetry from the Middle Ages to the present day. As for the proper dignity of the subject, Ramon Xirau's poem on the Arnolfini Portrait—one of the great icons of marriage—seems to suggest, in its final paradox, that the 'secrecy' and 'transparency' of the picture-space are at the same time qualities of the human relationship which it celebrates.

To re-create an existing work of art, as this last poem does, is one thing; to place one's poetic interpretation of everyday reality under the sign of an earlier artist or writer is another. I have already referred to the example of Ausiàs March; one might also think of the elder Breughel, a painter frequently evoked by Espriu and commemorated in a vivid poem by Francesc Parcerisas, where his simple aims and endless human curiosity are seen as an antidote to the 'dark night' of the present. This openness to the ordinary is at the root of Jordi Sarsanedas's poem addressed to Joan Salvat-Papasseit, the remarkable working-class poet, who died in 1924 at the age of thirty. Though Salvat is a more complex writer than the poem allows for, the qualities for which he is praised—his attention to the detail of city life and his celebration of the simplest moments of ordinary existence—are real enough, and the last three lines, as well as certain earlier images, refer directly to his own poems.

At the time it was written—the early 1950s—Sarsanedas's poem suggested a mixture of compassion and direct observation which was still rare in post-war Catalan poetry. Since then, the situation has changed: poems like those by Miquel Bauçà and Joan Colomines— modest in scope, yet unerringly accurate in their depiction of the lives of the under-privileged—are refreshingly common, and the same care for telling detail can be seen at work over a whole range of more or less 'personal' poems like Joan Perucho's clear-sighted reminiscence of his 1930s childhood or Vicent Andrés i Estellés's subtle charting of the passage from childhood to adolescence.

Such poems, moving as they do between the generations, are frequently set in a context of death and continuity. Thus the short sequence of poems by Rosa Leveroni I have already referred to balances with great honesty the fear of death against the Christian belief in immortality. Here, as in the much more agnostic poem by Agustí Bartra, one feels the weight of a lifetime's experience which nevertheless refuses to settle for certainties. For Bartra, clearly, the death of a poet—himself—who has celebrated life implies no break in the natural process or in the self-renewing power of the ancient myths. To others, however, his vision of a nature mourning its dead poet may seem over-romantic; human mourning, more often than not, goes with the sense of irretrievable loss expressed in Marta Pessarrodona's powerful though reticent poem 'In Memoriam'. Reticence here, indeed, is part of the poem's power: not only the fact that the dead poet is never named, but also the sense that the poem is making, with great economy, the only kind of public statement which can truthfully be uttered under the circumstances—a statement which, as the twist in the last line confirms, leaves intact the whole dimension of private mourning.

The reference to Aubrey's *Brief Lives* in this last poem reminds one of how often recent Catalan poets have reacted to English places and people. For some, like the Riba of the *Elegies de Bierville*, England (and in this case Ulster) is less a reality than a country of the mind, a creation partly of literature and partly of one's own ideals. For others, however, the sense is of a country experienced at first hand, in all its strangeness: the sculpture on which Marià Manent meditates belongs unmistakably to an *English* cathedral, just as, in

Narcís Comadira's poem, it is the understated quality of an English landscape that creates a mood which matches that of the anonymous student—a projection, perhaps, of the poet himself. For an English reader, the fascination of such poems lies partly in their ability to make the over-familiar seem strange. For the poets themselves, one imagines, the emphasis must fall rather differently: on the kind of awareness which makes it possible to construct a poem out of unfamiliar materials, and on the extension of sensibility this entails. And here, as Joan Margarit's poem 'Instantània' ('Snapshot') makes clear, 'constructing' may mean 'deciphering', as one moves beyond the conventional tourist image towards a more genuine understanding of the past.

The 'past', as this last poem seems to imply, lies somewhere between the objective evidence and the individual imagination which goes out to meet it. Alternatively, as in Xavier Amorós's poem about domestic happiness, the evidence itself may be personal: the deteriorating signs of a past which one may put behind, if only in the parenthesis of the family circle. Whatever the particular circumstances, it is clear that in such poems the idea of the 'past' serves as a way of focussing feelings which might otherwise remain elusive: a sense of the texture of one's own life, and of the unsuspected dimensions which may open up in one's daily living.

Much the same could be said of another abstraction—'nature'— which enters, however obliquely, into some of the poems towards the end of the anthology. None of these poems could be classed as 'nature poems' in the 19th-century Romantic sense, though several achieve their effect, it seems to me, by consciously exploiting the assumptions, and occasionally the imagery, of earlier, more conventional verse. Sometimes, as in the poem by Segimon Serrallonga, the traditional town-country contrast remains explicit, though here it involves a refusal to sentimentalize about the rural past. Àlex Susanna's poem, on the other hand, takes the characteristic Romantic celebration of nature—a nature conceived here largely in human terms—and re-casts it in such a way that the value of what is described is made to depend on the precariousness of its survival. Occasionally, the difference between these and more traditional poems of their kind is a matter of tone: the absence of comment and the sharply etched imagery in Tomàs Garcés's poem 'El Caçador' ('The Hunter'), or the individual voice which speaks through the poem by Salvador Oliva, where landscape—past, present and imaginary—plays a crucial part in the exploration of a personal relationship.

Nature, in all these poems, is relatively concrete: something which can be visualized and, more often than not, related to specific human situations. There are times, however, when the whole question of 'nature' becomes absorbed in speculation on the nature of reality itself. In the work of Foix, for instance, such speculation is literally a 'mirroring', since what is 'real' can only be reflected obliquely, in the verbal images and transformations of the poem. Inevitably, this affects the actual notion of a 'poem': if the limitations of language only allow certain aspects of reality to come into view, poetry, through its questioning of language, can at least suggest a kind of order which can never be formulated in rational terms. Thus a poem may cease to be a form of self-expression and become, in Christopher Middleton's phrase, an 'aperture upon being', a unique instrument of experience in which the 'modern' and the 'primitive' may coincide. Above all, perhaps, this means revising our sense of the poem's 'subject'. Thus we might say, as I myself have done, that Xirau's poem 'Jan Van Eyck' is about the Arnolfini Portrait; at the same time, the poem, like the actual picture, is a kind of *trompe l'oeil*: its short, incisive phrases reflect the changes of angle in the observer as he contemplates the picture both visually and mentally. As a result, the 'space' of the room is also a space in which certain connections are made, as they are in the poem itself; and if, at the end of the poem, this space is both 'secret' and 'transparent', this not only defines the quality of the ceremony described in the picture, as I suggested earlier, but also hints at the kind of effect the poem itself has tried to achieve.

This sense of a poem as a space whose nature changes under the pressure of the forces, both imaginative and conceptual, which meet in it, is central to the poetry of Pere Gimferrer. For Gimferrer, the roots of such a concept, clearly, lie in Symbolism, though a Symbolism filtered through the examples of Eliot, Wallace Stevens and Octavio Paz. Yet what strikes one most is the energy and intelligence with which he has attempted to write a genuinely 'modern' kind of poetry in Catalan, one which builds very deliberately on the strengths and qualities of the language itself, and on the unexplored possibilities of the existing poetic tradition. Like Foix, Gimferrer is acutely aware of the menacing aspects of reality and of the dangers involved in attempting to go beyond conventional categories. So, in 'Solstici' ('Solstice'), the inner conflict—the confrontation between man and reality—is conveyed in military images which suggest both a remote historical past and a timeless, self-renewing cosmic myth. In the last third of the poem, however, the highly metaphorical language becomes self-reflecting: words can suggest silence—the silence before language from which any true sense of the nature of reality must come—and writing itself may be a means of opposing the forces which threaten to destroy man in his search for reality. The poem itself, of course, expresses this much less abstractly; what is crucial, however, is the link which emerges between language and sexual love. Both, sooner or later, must come to terms with silence and the darkness of the unknown. And words, like plants, have their 'roots'; like the bodies of the lovers, they are capable of violence and conflict, but also of the kind of silent, unconscious knowledge which comes from their place in the natural process.

It is no coincidence that Gimferrer has written a fine study of the painting and sculpture of Joan Miró. Like Miró's 'universe of signs', so brilliantly evoked in the sestina by Joan Brossa, the co-ordinates of his poetic world are both infinitely suggestive and intensely local. Moreover, in Brossa himself (surely the most protean of contemporary Catalan writers) one finds a similar recognition that language itself— whether the language of art or of poetry—is an abstraction, and that terms like 'subject' and 'object' are, as a consequence, strictly relative. Brossa's own poem, in fact, shows, with astonishing directness, what this may imply. Of the six repeated rhyme-words, three (ratlles, taques, signes='lines', 'paint marks', 'signs') refer to painting, and three (vida, flames, sempre='life', 'flames', 'always') to energy and continuity. Thus the 'subject' of the poem is neither Miró nor his painting, but the way this painting works and the place of the artist in the operation. And by insisting on the two related sets of words, Brossa, like Miró himself, both resists the conventional idea of 'content' and suggests by analogy what for him is the nature of the world itself: something completely self-sufficient which it is impossible to translate into other terms.

Yet here there is a curious paradox: if the world, on this view, has no single, total meaning—it is simply itself—it is at the same time saturated with countless particular meanings. And, however universal his achievement, it is through the latter that the artist or the poet reveals his cultural allegiances. So part of Miró's vocabulary of signs, like his bird made from an actual hayfork, is rooted in a specifically Catalan context, just as the 'four flames' referred to in Brossa's poem correspond to the *quatre barres*, or 'four bars', of the Catalan coat-of-arms, and the 'crest' that they make suggests both a cock—the bird of resurrection—and the shape of the national headgear known as the *barretina*. So, too, in his own work, Brossa is able to draw on a wider range of popular material than any other modern Catalan writer: not merely types of verbal expression, but forms of popular art like the music-hall sketch or the illusionism of the conjurer.

In the end, however, it is to the language of poetry one returns, to the uses to which contemporary Catalan poets have put their own language, both literary and non-literary. Here again, it would be rash to generalize on the basis of a relatively small number of poems. Nonetheless, reading through the poems which appear in this anthology, I have been continually struck both by the energy and inventiveness of the writing and by what I can only describe as a certain playfulness, even in dealing with matters of life and death. Such playfulness by no means indicates a refusal of seriousness: more an avoidance of self-indulgence in establishing the kind of 'moral distance' of which Gabriel Ferrater speaks in the remark I quoted earlier. It is a quality best seen, I think, in practice: in certain poems by Pere Quart or by Ferrater himself, or in Joan Vinyoli's beautifully judged poem 'Passing-Shot', where the brilliance of the tennis metaphor almost triumphs over the good-humoured resignation of the speaker. In such poems, unpretentiousness is in no sense a negative quality; the inventiveness which more often than not goes with it is a large part of their attraction, no more so than when they are dealing with the kind of themes on which many less talented writers have foundered. Thus the poem which ends the anthology,

Martí i Pol's 'La Fi del Món' ('The End of the World') is both sobering and entertaining: a vision of a final cataclysm which deliberately avoids any theatrical effects, and achieves its climax through a loving and gently ironical re-creation of normality.

To suggest that there is something in the nature of the Catalan language which encourages this kind of poem would clearly be going too far, though perhaps only a Catalan reader could experience to the full both the surprise and the sense of recognition it entails. The same might be said, of course, of other, very different poems I have included. One sure sign of vitality in any country's poetry, after all, is the number of different directions it embodies at a given time, and I hope that, if nothing else, the present anthology will persuade readers, both Catalan and non-Catalan, of the achievement and continuing interest of one of the most fascinating bodies of poetry in any European language. If it does this, it will also of course have fulfilled—most appropriately, I believe—our more immediate aim: that of honouring our old friend and colleague Joan Gili on his 80th birthday.

ARTHUR TERRY

Postscript

I should also like to express my gratitude to those fellow-members of the Anglo-Catalan Society who collaborated in translating the poems. Without their assistance, it would scarcely have been possible to complete the present volume in time, and I can only say that it was a great pleasure to work with them.

ACKNOWLEDGEMENTS

The Anglo-Catalan Society wishes to place on record its appreciation of financial support received from Omnium Cultural and the Instituto de España en Londres. The patient collaboration and expertise of Pauline Climpson and her colleagues at the Sheffield Academic Press have smoothed the publication process. Grateful acknowledgement is made to them and to the following publishers: Edicions 62 (Barcelona), Editorial l'Estel (València), Editorial Crítica (Barcelona) Editorial Ariel (Barcelona), Editorial Lumen (Barcelona), Llibres del Mall (Barcelona), Edicions Proa (Barcelona), La Gaya Ciència (Barcelona).

Anthology

EL MÉS VELL DEL POBLE

Cap vent no mou el bri d'una esperança,
de cada núvol només cau neguit,
el destí s'enfondeix en malaurança,
potser la nit serà cent anys la nit.

El fat, però, no minva la frisança
pel que tant he volgut i beneït
si ma feblesa diu que ja s'atansa
l'adéu-siau del cos i l'esperit.

Potser ja massa dies he comptat
i en un recolze inconegut m'espera
la fi. Pugui jo caure, incanviat,

tot fent honor, per via dreturera,
amb ulls humits i cor enamorat,
a un esquinçall, en altre temps bandera.

JOSEP CARNER

The Oldest Man in the Village

No wind stirs the least wisp of hope, from every cloud descends nothing but disquiet, destiny sinks deep into adversity, perhaps the night will be night for a hundred years.

Yet fate does not lessen my impatience for what I have wished for and blessed so much even though my frailty declares that the time is approaching for body and spirit to bid each other farewell.

Perhaps I have exceeded my days and at some unfamiliar turn my end awaits me. Let me fall, unchanged,

still honouring, on a straight road, with moist eyes and loving heart, a tattered piece of cloth, that was once a flag.

[29]

A L'ENTRADA D'UNA ESTACIÓ SUBTERRÀNIA, LLIGAT DE
MANS I PEUS PER DUANERS BARBOSOS, VAIG VEURE
COM LA MARTA SE N'ANAVA EN UN TREN FRONTERER. LI
VOLIA SOMRIURE, PERÒ UN MILICIÀ POLICÈFAL SE'M VA
ENDUR AMB ELS SEUS, I VA CALAR FOC AL BOSC

Escales de cristall a l'andana solar
On passen trens de llum cap a platges obertes
Entre murs transparents i corals sarmentosos
I ocelles d'ull clarós en brogiment de brancs.

¿Ets tu, blanca en el blanc d'aquesta alba insular,
- Líquid l'esguard, atenta a músiques innates—
Que escrius adéus humits a la forest dels vidres,
Amb semença de nit per a un somni desclós?

AT THE ENTRANCE TO A SUBTERRANEAN STATION, TIED
HAND AND FOOT BY BEARDED CUSTOMS MEN, I SAW MARTA
LEAVING IN A FRONTIER TRAIN. I WANTED TO SMILE AT HER,
BUT A MANY-HEADED MILITIAMAN TOOK ME OFF WITH HIS
MEN, AND SET FIRE TO THE WOOD

Stairs of crystal on the solar platform where trains of light pass towards open
beaches between transparent walls and branching corals and bright-eyed
birds in a murmur of boughs.

Is it you, white in the white of this island dawn—your liquid gaze, alert to
inward music—who write moist farewells on the forest of windows, with
seed of night for an open dream?

[30]

Te'n vas enllà del goig, al ribatge encantat
Amb gegants embriacs a l'espluga gatosa
I falcons dissecats a les roques senyades,
A un mar petjat pels déus en els nocturns furtius.

No puc heure't, dorment, orb de llum i de ment,
Vestit com un infant, sense veu ni bagatge,
Entre tràmecs guardat per hostalers biformes;
Els passaports són vells i sangosos els cors.

T'emportes puigs i rius, i els estanys estel·lars
I fonts en bacs gelius en profundes valises;
Un guaita tenebrós, des del serrat en flames,
Em crida amb noms estranys i em fa que no amb les
     mans.

Onegen foramur banderes esquinçades.

                              Setembre de 1936

                    (*On he deixat les claus. . .*, VI)

                                        J.V. FOIX

You are going beyond joy, to the enchanted shore with drunken giants in the
thorny coves and dissected falcons on the cross-marked rocks, to a sea
trodden by gods in their furtive nocturnes.

I cannot reach you, sleeping, blind to light and thought, dressed like a child,
with neither voice nor luggage, guarded between hoes by double-formed
innkeepers; the passports are out of date and hearts are bleeding.

You take away with you in deep suitcases mountains and rivers and stellar
lakes and springs in icy hollows; a dark sentry, from the blazing mountain
ridge, calls me with strange names and says no to me with his hands.

Torn flags wave outside the walls.

LA VÍCTIMA

M'allunyava de tot, amics
i terra i cel. Vanament em cridàveu
quan era absent i nàufrag.
No em compadiu, sóc infeliç i alt
i gairebé sagrat, captiu d'aquest incendi
transfigurant la nit. Hi ha dies
llargs com la història dels homes.
És un instant el que ens salva.
Mai més no seré amb vosaltres.
Quan parlo, sento una veu estrafeta;
només quan callo, dic:
'Estremiu-vos, sóc la víctima marcada,
miro l'altar dels sacrificis'.

JOAN TEIXIDOR

The Victim

I became distant from everything, friends and earth and sky. Vainly you all cried out to me when I was gone and castaway. Do not pity me, I am unhappy and tall and almost sacred, a captive of this fire that transfigures the night. Some days are as long as the history of mankind. It is a single moment which saves us. No more shall I be with you. When I speak, I hear a voice disguised; only when I am silent do I say: 'Tremble all of you, I am the chosen victim, I behold the altar for the sacrifice'.

EL TEMPS ÉS FUM

Pobles perduts   al mig del temps que parla
del seu engany   de l'hora repetida
fins al final   reflex d'ella mateixa
   giravoltant

entorn d'un eix   esqueixats tots els altres
pels fets fingits   que omplen els fulls dels llibres
on s'han escrit   els somnis de la història
   els crits dels homes

que han existit   creient que ja vivien
i essent reals   destrossen rius, les tombes
dels seus antics   que són ells i no ho saben
   fins que morint

veurem ben clar   que el no-res senyoreja
el primer clam   la darrera paraula
i que ningú   ni jo ni els déus de marbre
   són més que fum

XAVIER BRU DE SALA

Time is Smoke

Peoples lost in the midst of time which speaks of its trickery, of the hour repeated till the end, a reflection of itself, rotating

around one axis, all the others rent apart by the bogus facts which fill the pages of books wherein have been written the dreams of history, the cries of men

who have existed believing that they lived and, being real, destroy rivers, the tombs of their forebears who are they themselves and who do not know it until dying

we shall clearly see that nothingness is lord over the first cry, the last word, and that no one, not I nor the marble gods, is more than smoke.

Ordenat, establert, potser intel·ligible,
deixo el petit món que duc des de l'origen
i des d'ell m'envoltà, car arriben de sobte
els neguitosos passos al terme del camí.
Concedida als meus ulls l'estranya força
de penetrar tot aquest gruix del mur, contemplo
els closos, silenciosos, solitaris
conceptes que van creant i enlairen
per a ningú les agitades mans del foc.
Ah, la diversa identitat davallada dels pous,
tan dolorós esforç per confegir i aprendre,
una a una, les lletres dels mots del no-res!
Ahucs del vent albardà entorn de la casa.
Vet aquí l'home vell, al davant de la casa,
com alça a poc a poc la seva pols
en un moment, àrid i nu, d'estàtua.
Terra seca després, ja per sempre
fora del nombre, del nom, trossejada
a les fondàries per les rels de l'arbre.

(*Llibre de Sinera*, XXXVIII)
SALVADOR ESPRIU

Ordered, established, perhaps intelligible, I leave the little world that I have carried with me from the beginning and which has ever since surrounded me, for suddenly the anxious steps come to the end of the road. Granted the strange power to penetrate the whole thickness of this wall, my eyes behold the closed, silent, solitary concepts that are created and raised up, for no one, by the restless hands of the fire. Ah, the diverse identity one has descended within the wells, such a painful effort to spell and learn, one by one, the letters of the words of nothingness! Shrieks of the wind clowning outside the house. Look how the old man, in front of the house, slowly raises his dust in the arid, naked moment of a statue. Afterwards dry earth, now for ever beyond number or name, broken up in its depths by the roots of the tree.

El cant em mena, i animals estranys
em volten purs, avesats a servir;
els reconec per fills del meu destí,
dolços al foc i fers als averanys.

Ja per la mort no em calen torsimanys:
és vida amunt que torna el meu camí;
si el que he après no fruitarà per mi,
el que he viscut no es comptarà per anys.

Sento absolut com el meu pas el món:
la llum revela el crit del cor pregon
i n'és la mida. ¿En què la saviesa

valdria? Folls actes meus que m'heu fet,
canilla ardent, us passo el magne plet;
i ens omplirem d'amor com d'una presa.

(Salvatge cor, XXIII)

CARLES RIBA

Song leads me on, and strange animals surround me, pure, accustomed to
serve; I recognize them as children of my destiny, mild before fire and fierce
to omens.

I no longer need interpreters for death: it is upwards in life that my path is
turning; if what I have learned will not bear fruit for me, what I have lived
will not be counted in years.

I feel the world is, like my footsteps, absolute: light reveals the cry of the deep
heart and is its measure. What would wisdom

be worth? Mad acts of mine which have made me, eager pack of hounds, I
entrust to you my great suit; and we shall fill ourselves with love, as with a
prey.

L'ESPERANÇA, ENCARA

En la meva donzellesa
ja et portava dins el pit,
Esperança, Confiança,
moviment de l'esperit!
«Sempre invoca l'esperança»
—diu un crític—«i de què?»
Mai no m'he sentit ben sola
que Esperança vol dir Fe.
I la casa se'm fa ampla
quan aquest vent s'hi expandeix,
alades paraules sento
veig l'arbre que refloreix.
En la meva viduesa
no vull ombres al meu dol.
He estat i sóc encara
dona que viu a ple sol.
La nit es lliga amb el dia
i et sé tan sovint amb mi!
que volo, somnio i sento
com si encara fos ahir.
Si el meu Carles m'enamora
—oh Esperanca!—
tu encara dius que sí.

1968

CLEMENTINA ARDERIU

Pujaré la tristesa dalt les golfes
amb la nina sense ulls i el paraigua trencat,
el cartipàs vençut, la tarlatana vella.
I baixaré les graus amb vestit d'alegria
que hauran teixit aranyes sense seny.

Hi haurà amor engrunat al fons de les butxaques.

MARIA-MERCÈ MARÇAL

[36]

Hope, still

When I was a girl you were there inside me already, Hope, Trust, the stirring of the spirit! 'She always invokes hope', says a critic, 'of what though?' I have never felt totally alone, for Hope signifies Faith. And my home feels too large for me when this wind spreads through it, I can hear winged words and see the tree turning green once more. Now I am a widow I want no shadows in my mourning. I have always been, and still am, a woman living in the sun's full glare. Night becomes intertwined with day and I know so often you are with me! I fly and dream and feel as if it were still yesterday. If my Carles still fills me with love—O Hope!—you still say yes.

I shall store grief up in the attic along with the doll with its eyes missing, the broken umbrella, the battered exercise-book and the old muslin. Then I shall come downstairs wearing the mantle of joy spun by madcap spiders.

Deep inside the pockets there will be crumbs of love.

TEMPS ENRERA

Deixa'm fugir d'aquí, i tornar al teu temps.
Trobem-nos altre cop al lloc de sempre.
Veig el cel blanc, la negra passarel·la
de ferros prims, i l'herba humil en terra
de carbó, i sento el xiscle de l'exprés.
L'enorme tremolor ens passa a la vora
i ens hem de parlar a crits. Ho deixem córrer
i em fa riure que rius i que no et sento.
Et veig la brusa gris de cel, el blau
marí de la faldilla curta i ampla
i el gran foulard vermell que dus al coll.
La bandera del teu país. Ja t'ho vaig dir.
Tot és com aquell dia. Van tornant
les paraules que ens dèiem. I ara, veus,
torna aquell mal moment. Sense raó,
callem. La teva mà sofreix, i fa
com aleshores: un vol vacil·lant
i l'abandó, i el joc amb el so trist
del timbre de la bicicleta. Sort

Time Was

Let me escape from here and go back to your time. Let's meet again in the usual place. I see the white sky, the black footbridge with thin metal struts, the humble grass on the cindery soil, and hear the whistle of the express. The enormous tremor passes beside us and we have to shout to hear one another. We give up, and it makes me laugh to see you laugh and not to hear you. I see your sky-grey blouse, the sea-blue of your short wide skirt and the big red scarf you wear round your neck. Your country's flag, as I said at the time. Everything is as it was that day. The words we spoke are coming back. And now—look—that bad moment returns. For no reason, we fall silent. Your hand is hurting, and behaves as it did then: it flaps uncertainly and drops, abandoned, to play with the sad sound of the bicycle bell. Luckily now,

que ara, com aquell dia, uns passos ferris
se'ns tiren al damunt, i l'excessiva
cançó dels homes verds, cascats d'acer,
ens encercla, i un crit imperiós,
com l'or maligne d'una serp se'ns dreça
inesperat, i ens força a amagar el cap
a la falda profunda de la por
fins que s'allunyen. Ja ens hem oblidat
de nosaltres. Tornem a ser feliços
perquè s'allunyen. Aquest moviment
sense record, ens porta a retrobar-nos,
i som feliços de ser aquí, tots dos,
i és igual que callem. Podem besar-nos.
Som joves. No sentim cap pietat
pels silencis passats, i tenim pors
dels altres que ens distreuen de les nostres.
Baixem per l'avinguda, i a cada arbre
que ens cobreix d'ombra espessa, tenim fred,
i anem de fred en fred, sense pensar-hi.

GABRIEL FERRATER

as on that day, those tramping metal feet bear down on us, and the excessive singing of the men in green, steel-helmeted, surrounds us, and a cry of command, like the malignant gold of a snake, rears up before us unexpectedly, and makes us hide our heads in the deep lap of fear until they have passed. Now we have forgotten ourselves. We are happy because they are going away. This movement without memory makes us find one another again, and we are happy to be here, the two of us, and it doesn't matter if we are silent. We can kiss. We are young. We feel no reverence for past silences, and we have other people's fears, which distract us from our own. We go down the avenue, and at every tree which covers us with deep shade, we feel cold, and go from chill to chill, unthinkingly.

Enc que sembli que no, tengué un principi.
Ara és tan natural, que no pareixen meves
totes les hores d'abans, d'abans que tu existissis.
M'ha entrat un tremolor, aquest capvespre
de setembre aigualit: és que pens que ens trobàrem
un dia, a un lloc, tu i jo: pogué no ocórrer.
Hauria estat senzill! Potser i tot aquell dia
t'hauria a tu semblat, des del teu món, perfecte,
i, des del meu, a mi, tot un noble transcórrer.
Res no hauria avisat del que perdíem.
Tu no series tu: potser ara hi hauria
una ombra vora meu patint el tràgic
destí d'haver de ser el que tu no series.

Although it may seem otherwise, it did have a beginning. It is so natural now,
that all those previous hours before you existed do not seem mine. A shiver
has come over me this rainy September evening as I think of how we met,
one day, in one place, you and I; it might not have happened. How easy that
might have been! Perhaps, even, that day might have seemed perfect to you,
from your world and to me, from mine, a most noble transit. Nothing could
have let us know what we were missing. You would not be you: maybe now
there would be a shadow near me suffering the tragic fate of having to be
what you would not be.

Talment com succeí, pogué no ocórrer.
Tant a tu com a mi, cadascú dins ca seva,
potser ens haurien dit «Has tengut un bon dia?»,
i hauríem dit que sí, espargint existència
com qui vessa un saler damunt la taula.
Just hi pens i tremol: aquests milers de dies,
aquest gaudi exultant, els guanys, les coses,
la salut, tants de llibres, els amics, la casa. . .,
sense haver existit tu,
tot seria tan curt, tan poca cosa. . .

(*Llibre de benaventurances*, XIX)

MIQUEL ÀNGEL RIERA

Just as it happened, it might not have happened. Each in our own homes, they might have asked you, as well as me, 'Had a good day, then?' and we would have said yes, scattering out existence like someone who knocks over a salt cellar on the table. I merely think of this and tremble: these thousands of days, this exultant joy, the gains, the things, health, so many books, friends, home. . ., if you had not existed, all would be so shallow, so paltry. . .

[41]

JAN VAN EYCK

A Manuel Duran

L'espai d'aquesta cambra, en el mirall
rodó del fons l'espatlla dels dos nuvis,
minucioses descripcions, presents,
minucioses.

Mirall rodó, llur doble? Més aviat, menuda
l'altre costat del cos, la no visible imatge.
Els dos nuvis no es miren, ella els ulls
baixos, ell, dret, inclinat una mica,
capell sobradament capell,
Hernaut Le Fin, de Lucca Arnolfi
(Itàlia rema, riu a riu, devers el Nord,
Flandes i Holanda baixen cap a Itàlia).

Jan Van Eyck

The space of this room, in the round mirror at the back the shoulders of the bridal pair, minute descriptions, present, minute.

Round mirror, their double? Rather, it diminishes the other side of the body, the non-visible image. The bridal pair do not look at one another, she with eyes lowered, he, erect, turning a little, hat excessively hat, Hernaut Le Fin, Arnolfi from Lucca (Italy rows, river by river, towards the North, Flanders and Holland descend to Italy.)

[42]

Arnolfi, braç alçat, promesa, amor distret?
Quietud de l'espai la llum penetra
per la finestra a l'esquerra, a la dreta
el llit vermell i vermell fosc en les cortines.
Aquesta noia, esverament,
vestida, verd oliva, i les mànigues blaves.
Les quatre mans immòbils es mouen, moviment
detingut aquest ball de les mans blanques.

En el mirall, rodó, d'esquena
(Flandes davalla cap a Itàlia),
l'espai secret i transparent
d'aquesta cambra.

RAMON XIRAU

Arnolfi, arm raised, a vow, distracted love? Quietness of space, the light
enters through the window on the left, on the right the red bed and the dark
red of the curtains. This girl, bewilderment, dressed in olive-green, with blue
sleeves. The four motionless hands move, this dance of the white hands a
suspended movement.

In the round mirror, seen from the back (Flanders descends to Italy) the
secret and transparent space of this room.

S'estimaren; saberen
la urgència del sexe, com les venes
poden en un moment omplir-se d'aigua
salobre, de sol d'estiu, de peixos
saltadors.
       S'amagaven
per la nit del pinar o per les tèbies
raconades de l'ombra.
Sentien, lassos,
la remor de l'oratge o el llunyaníssim
brogit de la ciutat.
En desvetllar-se l'endemà ella creia
que a l'alcova hi havia olor de roses,
i ell pensava el primer vers d'un poema
que mai no arribà a escriure.

They loved each other, you must know
V.A.

Once they loved each other; they knew the urgency of sex, and how veins can instantly fill up with salt water, summer sunshine, leaping fish.

They would hide among the night-time pine-woods, or in the lukewarm corners of darkness. Lying spent, they heard the wind murmuring or the far-distant roar of the city. On waking next morning she fancied she could smell roses in the bedroom, while he composed the first line of a poem he was never to write.

Les noces foren de pinyol vermell.
Tenen un fill notari a la península
i una filla amb promès.
Són gent d'allò que en diuen respectable.

Tornen a casa cap al tard, lentíssims,
assaborint cansadament la tarda.
Amb una punta de frisança, els ulls
se'ls perden qualque pic entre les branques
dels arbres del carrer, com si hi sotgessin
un reste de verdor o de carícia.
Miren els anys, el cel, les hores seques,
el rellotge i la pols. Caminen. Callen.

JOSEP M. LLOMPART

The wedding was a splendid affair. Now they have a son who's a lawyer on the mainland and a daughter who's engaged. They're what's known as respectable folk.

They come home late, very slowly, wearily relishing the evening. With a touch of impatience their eyes sometimes stray over the branches of the trees in the street, as though looking for some left-over greenness or caress. They watch the years, the sky, the dry hours, the clock, the dust. They walk in silence.

[45]

NOÈ

Noè mira, poruc, per l'ull de bou.
L'aiguat no amaina.
Ja es nega el pic més alt de la muntanya.
No es veu ni un bri de verd,
ni un pam de terra.

Senyor, per què no atures aquest xàfec?
Minva el gra i el farratge
i les bèsties es migren a les fosques;
totes—te'n faig l'aposta—
deuen pensar el mateix:
I mentrestant els peixos se la campen!
Jo tampoc no m'explico el privilegi.

Noah

Noah looks out, sheepishly, through the port-hole. The downpour is not abating. The mountain's highest top is now under water. There is not a strand of green to be seen, nor the smallest bit of ground.

Lord, why don't you turn off the tap? We're running out of corn and fodder, and the animals are wasting away in the darkness; all of them—I'll bet—must be thinking the same thing: 'It's lovely weather for fish!' I don't see either why they should have it so good.

[46]

Ja no donem abast tapant goteres;
i en dos indrets de la bodega
la fusta m'ha traït: traspua
a despit del betum.

Fa trenta dies que plou massa!

Noè cercava el cel per la lluerna
i veia la cortina espessa de la pluja.

La família, ho saps prou, no se'n fa càrrec.
Els fills em planten cara, rabiosos,
les nores xafardegen i no sirguen,
els infants, sense sol, s'emmusteeixen.
I la dona, ui la dona!
em fon, de pensament, amb la mirada.

We just can't cope now with all the leaks to be patched up; and there are two
places in the hold where the wood has let me down: water coming through in
spite of the pitch.

Thirty days of torrential rain!

Noah was peering through the sky-light: no sky, just the thick curtain of
rain.

The family, as you well know, don't understand. My sons turn and snap
angrily at me; the daughters-in-law just gossip and won't haul a rope; the
youngsters, without sunshine, grow pale and wan. And the wife—Gawd, the
wife! If looks could kill...

[47]

Tanta humitat no em prova:
garratibat de reuma,
què valc, Senyor?
I, a més, el temps pesa qui-sap-lo:
ja en tinc sis-cents de repicats!

Prou mullader, Jahvè, repensa't!
Que el bastiment, de nyigui-nyogui,
poc mariner, sortí d'una drassana
galdosa, a fe!
i el costellam grinyola, es desajusta.

No m'ennaveguis més, estronca
les deus de la justícia
i engega el sol de la misericòrdia!
Ja fóra hora d'estendre la bugada!

All this dampness is doing me no good: crippled with rheumatics, what use am I, Lord? And how the time drags: six-hundred sure is a ripe old age!

We've been drenched enough, Jehovah: give us a break! Sure, this old tub, hardly fit to put to sea, must have come from a cock-eyed shipyard, and that's a fact! It's creaking and coming apart at the ribs.

Don't keep me at sea any longer; stop the gushing waters of justice and light up the sun of mercy! It's about time we could hang out the washing!

Ben cert que ets Tu qui fa i desfà les coses;
i per amor de tu suportaré el que calgui.
Només volia dir-te
            —i sé per què t'ho dic—
que aquest país no és per a tanta pluja,
i el llot no adoba res:
cria mosquits i lleva febres.
Caldrà refer els conreus i escarrassar-se.
Som quatre gats malavinguts
i me n'estic veient una muntanya...

Vingué aleshores un tudó tot blanc,
però ensutzat de colomassa,
i s'aturà a l'espatlla dreta
del vell senyor almirall,
el qual, amb la mà plana,
oferí quatre veces a l'ocell amansit.
En aquell temps ningú no s'estranyava
de res.
            Vegeu la Bíblia.

PERE QUART

There's no doubting that You are the maker and the unmaker of all things; and
for love of you I'll put up with anything. I just wanted to tell you—and I've got
my reasons for speaking out—that this country can't take so much rain, and
mud is no good for anything: it just breeds mosquitos and diseases. We'll have
to get the crops going again and put our backs into it. We're a sparse and
motley crew and it'll be an uphill struggle...

Then came a pure white dove, but soiled from being cooped up for so long,
and settled on the right shoulder of the old admiral who stretched out an
open hand to give the meek bird a few grains of vetch. In those days nobody
was surprised about anything.

Just take a look in the Bible.

HOMENATGE A BRUEGEL EL VELL

En aquesta nit nostra té cada cop més interès parlar
tots junts de la carícia dels vestits que desllinden
l'home del món, la carn de l'instrument de treball.
Perquè estem recordant el vell Bruegel i els seus
primaverals blaus que allunyen els camps
i l'or polsós del blat i dels capells de palla,
els ramats indòcils com fulles de coure
i el glaç i la neu del poble que pateix
l'hivern i la injustícia d'una terra
feta a la mida d'una llei senyorial.
(Recordeu que va néixer el 1528 a la ciutat de Breda.)

Homage to Breughel the Elder

In this night of ours it becomes of ever greater interest to speak, all together,
of the caress of the clothes that divide man from the world, the flesh from the
instrument of work. Because we are recalling old Breughel and his springlike
blues which distance the fields and the dusty gold of the wheat and of the
straw hats, the stubborn flocks like copper leaves, and the ice and snow of the
village suffering the winter and the injustice of an earth made to the measure
of a feudal law. (Remember, he was born in 1528 in the city of Breda.)

Parlem de l'exemple del vell Bruegel
perquè l'amor al treball i a la vida de l'oci,
amb camperols sorruts que juguen a bitlles
i patinadors que rellisquen i cauen de cul,
té les expressions més belles en la mà
del mestre flamenc. En aquesta nit fosca
en un minso país com el nostre encara s'esmunyen
idealistes cabòries del que hauria d'ésser i no és.
I ell, Bruegel el vell, mort en plena verema,
agafà uns colors i amb els dits del cor
ens proposà la història de tota l'estètica:
'jo pinto la vida dels homes'.
Descobriu-vos el cap.

FRANCESC PARCERISAS

Let's talk about the example of old Breughel, since love of work and of the life of leisure, with sullen peasants playing skittles and skaters who slip and land on their backsides, finds its most beautiful expression at the hand of the Flemish master. On this dark night in a frail country like ours, idealistic worries about what ought to be and isn't still slip through. And he, Breughel the Elder, who died at the height of his powers, took up some colours and, with the fingers of his heart, set before us the history of the whole of aesthetics: 'I paint the life of mankind'. Take your hats off to him.

PRIMERA LLETRA ESCRITA AL CAPVESPRE

Petites prades sota un cel intacte i rutilant
solcat per globus de colors, paraules d'or massís,
sospirs de fronda exhausta, imatges de gent difunta
que es perderen per sempre en aquest aire immòbil.
No, no ha estat així tota la vida, perquè, llavors,
freqüentment, distant i molt discreta, la dama
de color de turquesa feia ganxet, arrecerada,
i Lluís, el meu cosí, vestit de mariner, corria
darrera la bicicleta del somni, i queia molt sovint.
Això era vers l'any mil nou-cents trenta, l'aroma
de les coses era una altra, i una taronja tenia
el gust de sol. Sé perfectament el que equival a un home.

Però recordo el passeig que anava al misteriós país,
les malalties, la joia, el tresor amagat, la ploma groga,
els plors, l'aire innocent del meu fabulós, ignot,
remot, i per sempre perdut, país de les meravelles.

JOAN PERUCHO

First Letter Written at Dusk

Tiny meadows under an unblemished sparkling sky furrowed by coloured
balloons, words in solid gold, sighs like limp fronds, images of people now
dead who vanished for ever in this still air. No, life was not always like that,
for then, quite often, the turquoise-coloured lady, so distant and discreet, sat
with her crochet well protected, and Lluís, my cousin, in his sailor-suit, ran
along behind the dream bicycle, stumbling time and time again. All this was
around nineteen thirty, things smelled different then, and an orange tasted of
sunshine. I know perfectly well what is on a par with a man.

But I remember the path leading to the mysterious land, the illnesses, the
joy, the hidden treasure, the yellow pen, the tears, the innocent air of my
fabulous, unknown, remote wonderland, now gone for good.

[52]

Els diumenges, a la tarda, al pobre barri
de Santa Marina, a la menuda rambla sense ocells,
amb arbres bruts de fums, amb cinema de dues pessetes,
al bar *La Parra*, amb el tocadiscs llogat, ballen
els fills dels obrers, sota la benigna mirada
de les mares grasses.
Els nois estrenyen les noies davant la setmana
de por que se'ls ve al damunt. Els nois no parlen.
Les noies somriuen i s'abandonen amb mesura
als braços i al ritme del fox. Les parelles
alternen, tristes, i s'evadeixen. . . '. . .fins a l'eternitat!!!'
El cel és gris, com sempre, damunt el pobre, brut barri
de Santa Marina i damunt les parelles
que s'evadeixen fins a l'eternitat. . .

MIQUEL BAUÇÀ

On Sunday evenings, in the poor quarter of Santa Marina, on the tiny birdless avenue, with sooty trees and a two-peseta cinema, at the *Grapevine* bar, the workers' children dance to a hired record-player, beneath the kindly gaze of their fat mothers. The boys hold the girls tight before the dreadful week which is almost on top of them. The boys don't speak. The girls smile and surrender themselves decorously to their arms and to the rhythm of the fox-trot. The couples alternate, sadly, and escape. . . 'to eternity!!!' The sky is grey, as always, over the poor, dirty quarter of Santa Marina and over the couples who are escaping to eternity. . .

POSTAL DE SARRIÀ

Veus passar el món un diumenge a la tarda
al teu balcó. Només tens els ulls vius
i et fas l'absent. Tan sols un lleu cruixir
del teu vestit et fa tornar els records
amb què has omplert armaris amb olor
de fruita vella. Imperceptiblement
gires la mà. Et voleien les pors
i et fan l'ullet. T'has fet gran, potser massa
al teu desig. El món t'és un sol baix.
Fan ball a plaça. Els crits els sents davant
però no et mous. Els sons t'arriben morts.
Els veus passar com veus que passo jo
pel teu davant: com un no-res obscur.
No sóc al teu record ni hi és el ball.
Tu ja només tens son. Ets una estàtua
que han tret del seu jardí i l'han posat
en un balcó: un núvol blanc que alena.

JAUME VALLCORBA PLANA

Postcard from Sarrià

You watch the world going by on a Sunday afternoon from your balcony.
Only your eyes are alive, the rest of you switches off. Just a slight rustle of
your clothes brings back the memories with which you have filled wardrobes
with the scent of old fruit. Imperceptibly you turn your hand over. Your fears
flutter up, winking at you. You have grown old, perhaps too old for your own
liking. The world to you is a sun low down. They are dancing in the square.
You can hear loud voices out there but you do not move. The sounds are
dead when they reach you. You see them go by as you see me passing before
you: like some dark nothingness. I am not in your memory, neither is the
dance. You now are just sleepy. You are a statue which has been moved from
its garden and placed on a balcony: a white cloud breathing.

GOIG DEL CARRER

La joia pura del carrer
ens va reblir les mans de tendres grapats d'aigua
i ens rèiem, bovament ens rèiem,
i a tots els músculs era l'aigua viva del goig,
vinguda entre les herbes i les llebres.
Anàvem sense cap motiu,
desitjant bona nit al matrimoni vell
i prement nostres cossos calladament, en veure
aquella jove mare,
donant el pit al fill. . .
Viure ens era un regal,
un teuladí de fang amb dos plomes pintades de fugina,
un cavalcar corsers de cartó, grocs i verds,
com en una sardana de joguet,
fent-nos senyals, dient-nos: *Adéu, adéu, amor! Mai no
t'oblidaré!*

Delight in the Street

The sheer joy of the street filled our hands with tender clutches of water, and
we laughed, we mooed with laughter, and in all our muscles we felt the living
water of delight, sprung from between grasses and hares. We wandered along
aimlessly, saying goodnight to the old couple and silently pressing our bodies
together on seeing a young mother with a child at her breast. . . Living was a
present we had been given, a pottery sparrow with two feathers picked out in
the colours of truancy, a charge of horses on a roundabout, yellow and green,
as in a toy *sardana*, when we waved to each other saying, 'Good-bye, good-
bye, my love! I'll think of you always'.

La vida ens era una sorpresa,
una granota viva a la butxaca,
una cúpula enorme de cristall,
un silenci, un desig rabent, un estupor,
un rellotge parat, que Algúens havia
donat perquè a la fi el poguéssem obrir,
com des de nins volíem,
i no tenia res interessant a dins. . .
I ens tornàrem a riure!
El temps estava en l'aire. I allargàvem les mans
cercant grapats de temps. Però el temps tampoc no era. . .
Només era la joia del carrer.
I els crits
     —Gol! Gol!—
dels infants que jugaven
al futbol en sortir de l'escola. . .

VINCENT ANDRÉS I ESTELLÉS

Life was all surprise to us, a live frog in a pocket, an enormous glass dome, a silence, a raging desire, stupor, a stopped watch that someone had given us so that finally we could look inside, like we had wanted to since we were very small, and inside there was nothing interesting to see. . . And we burst out laughing again! It felt as though time was in the air. And we were reaching out, grasping for handfuls of time. But there was just no such thing as time. . .! All there was was the joy of the street. And the shouts—*Goal! Goal!*—of children playing football on their way home from school.

Era pels volts de mitjanit,
l'hora que el grill
i les estrelles
comencen de parlar.

Vora la mar,
quasi al sorral,
una munió de barracots.

Era l'estiu.

L'oreig
duia l'aroma de salobre
i una lleu humitat.

De dins de les barraques,
amb teulada de llauna,
massa calor
foragitava tot vivent.

La lluna il·luminava
aquella gent
que jeien pels carrers.

It was around midnight, when the cricket and the stars begin their dialogue.

By the sea, almost on the strand, a collection of shacks.

It was summer.

The breeze bore on it the scent of brine and a touch of humidity.

The unbearable heat indoors drove every living creature out of the shacks with their tin roofs.

The moon shone on those folk as they lay in the streets.

Ningú no s'estranyà
d'aquell
qui caminava entre els secrets
de llurs intimitats.

Perquè en la pau
de mitjanit,
fatigats de la lluita i del viure
només, només volien
aquella trista llibertat
de dormir al carrer,
lliures de la calor
i dels insectes.

Només una petita llibertat:
una mica de fresca
en una nit d'estiu
calorosa i humida.

JOAN COLOMINES I PUIG

No one bothered about the passer-by strolling among the secrets of their private lives.

For in the midnight calm, worn out by the struggle and just by living, all they wanted was that poor wretched freedom to sleep in the street, released from the heat and the insects.

Just a little freedom: a breath of cool air on a hot and humid summer's night.

PETIT MONUMENT A JOAN SALVAT-PAPASSEIT

Planerament invoco el teu fantasma
amb mots planers dels versos que ens deixares
quan caigueres al clot de la teva esperança.
No per inflar els meus d'una noble bufera
et dic de tu, sinó com als companys.
Sóc vell com la teva mort,
sóc jove com la teva vida.
Un mestre, tu no ho ets. Els doctes (reverència!)
t'assenyalen vergonyes amb les busques d'acer,
i qui els contradiria?
Però vares donar una llum a la gent,
però vares tocar-la d'una llum a la cara
que s'ha fet veritat,
i la nostra ciutat
no fóra ben bé la d'ara,
si no haguessis parlat dels carrers de l'esclat
del bon dia que fa,
de l'encant de les feines.

Little Monument to Joan Salvat-Papasseit

I invoke your spirit simply with simple words from the poetry that you left us when you fell into the grave of your hope. It's not to swell up my own with any noble airs that I speak familiarly to you, but just to talk to you as a friend. I am old as your death, I am as young as your life. A master you are not. The erudite (due respect please!) pick out your failings with their pointers of steel and who would contradict them? But you gave a light to the people, but you touched their faces with a light which has become real and our city would not really be as it is now, had you not spoken of the street, of the brightness of the beautiful day that it is, of the charm of every job.

Fa anys que vas morir. I ara estic content
del teu fantasma jove.
Així puc anar amb tu sense cap compliment
pels camins i els treballs d'aquesta primavera
que és la vida i la mort eternament.
El rovell s'ha menjat l'esfera del cafè
que l'adroguer voltava, i el foc de Sant Joan
els grans cistells de vímet.
Passen cotxes enormes com vaixells de platxeri
i d'altres menudets com esclops d'alumini.
Al port hi ha noves llums, de nit, i dues torres
de ferro.
Ja són velles, les torres, ja cauen.
Fa tant que tu ets mort, i han passat tantes coses!

Però encara
que l'irradiador del port tingui ara radar,
són iguals les gavines,
i els vestits lluminosos de les noies d'estiu,
i els besos a la gorja,
i els colors de les hores que llisquen pels carrers,
i el groc de les taronges,
i tu que amb nosaltres veus
com és bo tot:
i la Vida
i la Mort.

JORDI SARSANEDAS

You died years ago. And now I'm glad of your young spirit. In this way, I can walk with you, without ceremony, through the street and labours of this spring which is life and death eternally. Rust has eaten away the coffee grinder that the grocer turned and midsummer night's fire, the great wicker baskets. Enormous cars go past like pleasure cruisers and smaller ones like aluminium clogs. In the port there are new lights, at night, and two iron towers. They're old now, the towers, and are falling down. You've been dead for so long and so many things have happened.

Yet even though the port beacon has got radar now, the seagulls are the same, and the luminous dresses of the girls of summer, and the kisses on the throat, and the yellow of the oranges, and you who, with us, see how good it all is: Life and Death.

Tot allò que diem
ha estat dit per un altre.
Ho sabíem de sempre.
A cada pas que fem,
se'ns oblida l'ofici
i cada vers ens sobta,
tot i tenir-lo dintre.
El secret és saber-ho,
talment com quan sentim
des de llocs oposats
el galop dels cavalls
per les rieres seques.
Aleshores cal prémer
(dins la vall plena d'ecos)
el llibre ben obert
contra la pana: un llamp
es clavà al cor cremat
del vidre. . ., confirmem.

FELIU FORMOSA

Everything we say has been said by someone else. We always knew that.
With each step we take, we forget our trade and each line of verse surprises
us, even though we have it inside us. The secret is to know this, as when we
hear coming from different directions the sound of horses galloping down the
dry river beds. Then's the time to press the book (in the echo-filled valley)
wide open against the corduroy; a flash of lightning has embedded itself in
the scorched heart of the glass. . ., we confirm the result.

SONET A AUSIAS MARCH

Com soferràs los mals qui et són davant?

Poeta enter, ensenyes el dolor
que hi ha en el fons de tota vida humana:
la teva veu ressona com campana
des del passat a l'esdevenidor.

Poeta amic, quin secret les paraules
serven avui que ens puguin concitar?
Tens el poder de fer sobresaltar
els nostres ulls embadalits pels saules.

Poeta aspriu, difícil de tenir,
card entre llirs, en el que vagis dir
¿descobrirem un dia el teu misteri?

Però què hi fa? El que importa és el setge
per tu bastit, Ausiàs March, heretge,
que ha perdurat al mateix encanteri.

FRANCESC VALLVERDÚ

Sonnet to Ausiàs March
How will you bear the troubles in store for you?'

Complete poet, you show up the pain that lies in the depths of every human life: your voice resounds like a bell ringing out from the past to the future.

Dear poet, what secret do words hold today that they can still stir us? You have the power to shock our eyes as they gaze distractedly at the willows.

Rough-diamond poet, difficult to handle, thorn among the lilies, shall we one day, in what you said, discover your mystery?

But what matter? What is important is the siege that you laid, Ausiàs March, you heretic, which has outlived enchantment itself.

[62]

CINC POEMES DESOLATS

. . .cuyd'haver port en la plaja deserta

AUSIÀS MARCH, XCII, 57

I

Com un gorg sense llum ni remors d'aires tendres,
sospirós pels estels i l'esclat de les ales
que mai no el signaran i es morfon lentament
sense un crit d'esperança. . .
Així em passen els jorns, orfe d'aquell meu cant
que posava clarors en l'aspror del camí.
Si l'amor fou neguit, m'era dolça l'espina
i com ocell orbat, el dolor m'era càntic.
Ara el feix de l'amor, damunt el cor cansat
és només solitud
de la flama feroç devorant en silenci
la vida que es consum lluny de tu, lentament,
sense un crit d'esperança. . .

Five Desolate Poems

. . .he imagines there is a harbour on the empty beach
AUSIAS MARCH, XCII, 57

I

Like a gorge without daylight or the whisper of gentle breezes, yearning for
the stars and the flash of wings which will never leave their mark there,
slowly wasting away without a single cry of hope. . . So do the days pass me
by, bereft of my one-time song that cast patches of light on the rough track. If
love was frustration, still its thorn was sweet to me and, like a blinded bird,
pain led me to sing. But now the burden of love pressing down on a worn-out
heart is merely loneliness, a fierce flame which silently devours a life
consumed far from you, slowly, without a single cry of hope. . .

[63]

II

Com l'animal ferit, morir ben sola
de cara al cel només, dins la malesa
abastada amb dolor, fora recances
d'uns lligams ja trencats, passat el fàstic
del darrer desengany, trista metzina
necessària a la mort. . . Morir ben sola,
els ulls de bat a bat a l'alegria
del gran despullament. Dolç oblidar-se
del dard que m'aterrà, misèria d'altri
però meva també. Morir ben sola,
estalviar el meu crit en la tenebra:
Certa de la Claror. . .

II

Like a wounded beast, to die alone, facing nothing but the sky, in the
undergrowth it hurt so much to reach, beyond regret for ties now broken,
past loathing for the final disappointment, the sorry poison that death
requires. . . To die alone, eyes open wide on the joy of this great divestment.
Sweet forgetfulness of the shaft which felled me, wretchedness for others, but
also for me. Die alone, sparing my cry in the darkness: certain of the
Light. . .

III

Cor desolat, vela al vent de la tarda,
passa rabent aquest freu de sirena.
Si l'has vençut, sempre més el teu somni
en sentirà la impossible enyorança.

Cor desolat, dins sos ulls qui fos nàufrag
sense records de la pàtria llunyana.
Timons ardents de les hores enceses
sense ponents ni desigs de cap alba.

Cor desolat, nua roca deserta,
presa del vent i del sol i de l'aigua.
La llibertat si ara és plor serà càntic,
cor desolat, en la vida més alta.

III

Desolate heart, a sail billowing in the evening breeze, pass swiftly through the siren's strait. If once you sail beyond it, you will evermore dream of it with impossible nostalgia.

Desolate heart, oh to be a shipwrecked sailor in your eyes, free from memories of the distant homeland. Ardent helms of the glowing hours without sunsets or desire for any dawn.

Desolate heart, bare empty rock, the prey of the wind, sun and water. Freedom may be sorrow now but will become a hymn of joy, oh desolate heart, in that higher life.

IV

Pedra i l'udol del vent damunt la pedra
si s'alça alguna veu, sinó el silenci
de l'implacable sol bevent-se l'aigua
en la més fonda deu. Ales sinistres
dels corbs esgarriats. No hi ha el misteri
de l'alba, del ponent... La llum, la roca
castigada pel foc... Aquesta pedra
et vol cridar. Senyor, crida ta pluja
i Tu no li respons. Perduda, sola,
fins a l'entranya roc; què espera encara?
Digues, on ets, Senyor...

IV

Stone and the wind howling over the stone, if any voice is raised, else the
silence of the unremitting sun drinking in water from the deepest spring.
Stray crows with their sinister wings. The mystery of dawn, of sunset, no
longer exists... Light, rocks ravaged by fire... This stone wants to cry out to
you. Lord, it cries for your rain and You ignore it. Lost, alone, stone through
and through; what can it still be hoping for? Tell me, Lord, where are
you...

V

Rera del mur, segures,
sento velles paraules
cridant imperioses
el retorn a la terra,
antiga pàtria trista.
La meva passa immòbil
s'ha arrelat en la fosca.
Els ulls àvids reclamen
la dolça claror seva.
El mur la defenia
i el cor, covard, no gosa
emprendre la conquesta.

ROSA LEVERONI

V

Behind the wall, I can hear old words in safety loudly demanding to return to their country, back to the ancient sad homeland. My motionless passage has taken root in the darkness. Eager eyes seek to claim its sweet brilliance. The wall protected it and the cowardly heart does not dare to embark on the conquest.

Quan de mi, finalment, sols quedaran les lletres
posades com ocells damunt els cables tensos
dels esperits fidels als himnes de la vida,
un martell plorarà per la llum apagada.
El dia portarà corones de mimoses.
Potser hi haurà perdó en la mar que no calla.
El sol tindrà a la boca la seva sempreviva
i noves veus diran l'alegria de l'aigua.
El vent devastarà el fanal i l'estàtua.
Els estius lluiran les seves bruses grogues
i el bastó blanc del cec sonarà als carrers grisos.
Entre les roques aspres i als boscos de les ànimes,
Orfeu seduirà les anònimes bèsties.
Vindran els plenilunis a fer fremir les verges
que esperaran l'amor entre els grills i l'acàcia.
Jo ja no tindré rostre. A mes oïdes d'herba,
el temps farà dringar un cascavell d'estrelles. . .

AGUSTÍ BARTRA

When of me, finally, only the letters remain, perched like birds on the taut
wires of the spirits faithful to life's hymns, a hammer will weep for the light
that has gone out. Day will wear mimosa wreathes. Perhaps there will be
forgiveness in the never silent sea. The sun will hold in its mouth its
everlasting flower, and new voices will speak of the joy of water. The wind
will lay waste the street lamp and the statue. The summers will show off
their yellow blouses, and the blind man's white stick will sound on the grey
streets. Among the rough rocks and in the woods of the souls Orpheus will
seduce the anonymous beasts. The full moons will come to make the virgins
shiver as they wait for love among the crickets and acacia. I shall no longer
have a face. Time will make a bell of stars tinkle in my ears of grass.

IN MEMORIAM

No s'arnen els vestits;
s'esfilagarsa, però, el dolor
i un buit afrós troba el seu lloc depredador
quan, a la fi, s'acaba.

El poeta viu en qui l'admira,
quan l'home ja l'han fet servir
tots i, com és sabut, només
pols, memòries tènues, dolors
silents, en resten.

In Memoriam

The clothes do not get moth-ridden; the grief, however, becomes frayed and a dreadful vacuum finds its predatory place when the former finally ceases.

The poet lives on in those who admire him, when everyone has done with the man himself and, as we know, all that remains of him is dust, vague memories, silent pangs.

Penso en el que digué el vell Aubrey
—pobre i polsós en unes golfes de Bloomsbury—:
«quan un home de saber mor,
quantes coses ens són robades».
I Aubrey parlava de Shakespeare.

Els llibres d'història són un vici
que totes les policies accepten.
I viure és una manera de combatre
les arnes, les recances a la matinada.
La veritat, però, és una altra.

MARTA PESSARRODONA

I recall what old Aubrey said—poor and dusty in a Bloomsbury garret—
'When a man of knowledge dies, how many things are stolen from us'. And
Aubrey was speaking of Shakespeare.

History books are a form of vice accepted by all police forces. And living is a
means of fighting off the moths, the regrets that come in the early hours. The
truth, however, is different.

PRIMAVERA ANGLESA

No és que un sol massa feble
filtrant-se entre aquests oms de fulla tendra
pugui fer-me enyorar primaveres més clares:
aquí l'herba esplendent i el vellut de la molsa
tenen llum permanent
i bé poden
recolzar passions amb perfum de jacint
o amb els pètals alats dels narcisos.
Lent, el canal discorre, quasi immòbil,
com si volgués quedar-se
la imatge pacient del pescador,
la trèmula frisança del bedoll,
o el núvol.

English Spring

It is not that a feeble sunlight filtering through these soft-leaved elms can make me yearn for brighter springs: here the shiny grass and the velvet moss have a permanent gleam and can well sustain passions with the scent of hyacinth or with the winged petals of the daffodils. Slowly, the canal glides along, almost motionless, as if wishing to hold on to the patient image of the angler, the tremulous shimmer of the birch, or the cloud.

Res del món no existeix fora d'això,
fora d'aquesta
lentitud aparent
amb què se'n van les coses.
(Que punyent ens semblarà el dolor
amb aire nou i ocells entre els lilàs.)
Però el món va seguint el seu camí.
L'estudiant
ha tancat el seu llibre i es distreu
sembla que amb un bri d'herba.
Però és tot el món que el distreu,
la transparent cortina de sofriments i afectes
que li priva
de llançar-se al somriure esplendorós
d'uns instants que sap breus i que, amb tot,
són els únics feliços.

NARCÍS COMADIRA

Nothing on earth exists beyond this, beyond this apparent slow motion with which things recede. (How sharply shall we feel the pain when the air is new and there are birds among the lilacs.) But the world continues on its same old way. The student has closed his book and seems distracted by a blade of grass. But what distracts him is the whole world, the transparent curtain of suffering and feeling that prevents him from breaking through to the radiant smile of instants which he knows are brief and which, even so, are the only time of happiness.

EL DAVID DE LA CATEDRAL
DE SALISBURY

Aeri, en la grisor de la pedra, en el vent,
entre els crits de les gralles iròniques, t'inclines,
abstret damunt de l'arpa, a la música ardent.
Però una herba se't mou sobre les cordes fines.

Ara és verda i menuda aquesta arpa, que duu
al teu cos mineral una trèmula saba
del juny assolellat i feliç, mentre tu
escoltes, i qui sap si una abella et besava.

Més enlaire que el cedre, entre dos àngels greus,
no veus enamorats a la prada, el tord lliure
que xiula sobre l'herba dels morts. I vora els teus
brins de música, lluny, t'endevino el somriure.

MARIÀ MANENT

The David of Salisbury Cathedral

Aloft, in the greyness of the stone, in the wind, amid the cawing of ironic
crows, you bend, engrossed over your harp, to the passionate music. But a
weed brushes across your slender strings.

Now it is green and small, this harp that brings into your mineral body the
tremulous sap of sunny, happy June, as you listen, and perhaps a bee kissed
you.

Higher than the cedar, between two solemn angels, you do not see lovers in
the meadow, the unfettered thrush that sings over the lawns of the dead. And
close to your wisps of music, in the distance, I sense that you are smiling.

[73]

INSTANTÀNIA

Espais d'enyor perfan l'arquitectura
dels carrers frescos amb olor de mar
i oratge d'uns diumenges al matí
que ens deturàvem als portals ombrosos
per admirar una escala al fons d'un pati
o la senzilla dignitat d'un arc.
Sovint havíem d'enlairar l'esguard
fins als vestigis d'un esgrafiat
que, calmosos, anàvem desxifrant
mentre a Santa Maria repicaven
les altes campanades que se senten,
avui encara, al fons de l'estuc blau.
on componem els frescos del passat.

JOAN MARGARIT

Snapshot

Spaces of nostalgia complete the architecture of the cool streets smelling of
sea and wind some Sunday mornings as we stopped at shady portals to
admire a stairway on the far side of a courtyard or the simple dignity of an
arch. Often we had to raise our eyes to the remains of a carved inscription
that we leisurely deciphered while from the church of Santa Maria rang out
the lofty peals of the bells that can still be heard, even today, in the depths of
the blue stucco, where we piece together the frescoes of the past.

CASES AMB GRANS ARBRES

Encara hi ha cases amb grans arbres
on poder passejar els capvespres,
temps d'aïllament tranquil i pausat,
temps d'enyor i somnieig:
temps per mirar el mar dòcil
i sortir a passejar, sol o bé en silenci,
per algun camí poc fressat des d'on mirar
les llums del dia i la nit entrecreuar-se,
i perdre's un, a la fi, en la llunyania.
Escoltar la terra, les seves olors,
el seu ardent missatge,
freturós potser de nosaltres, d'algú tan sols . . .

Houses with Tall Trees

There are still houses with tall trees where you can wander in the evening, a time for peaceful unhurried withdrawal, a time for nostalgia and dreams; for watching the calm sea and strolling, either alone or in silence, down some quiet path, where the lights of day and night can be watched as they overlap, and finally lose yourself in the distance. Listening to the earth with its smells and its fervent message, which might, perhaps, need us, or anyone at all. . .

Sempre he pensat que era injust, injust del tot,
que ningú no gaudís d'una lluna plena al mar a l'hivern,
o d'aquell cel florit i palpitant en les nits d'alta muntanya,
o del tendre crit dels camps nus a la primavera,
o bé del silenci excessiu i poderós que embolcalla algun
cami de rastre ja perdut . . .
Sort, sort que encara hi ha cases amb grans arbres
on poder dissipar-se els capvespres:
no pensar en res,
acostar-se una mica a la terra,
i, ben a prop de la mort però sense témer-la,
retreure's de tot, sí, vagament de tot . . .

ÀLEX SUSANNA

I have always thought it was unfair, really unfair, that no-one can enjoy a full moon at sea in winter, or that blossoming throbbing night sky of the mountains, or the tender cry of bare fields in spring, or yet the overbearing powerful silence that shrouds an erased track . . .

How lucky, how lucky there are still houses with tall trees where you can while away the evenings: thinking of nothing, and draw a little closer to the earth, then, standing next to death, but unafraid of it, lightly slip away, ah yes, from it all.

Ara sóc a la falda de casa.
Una sentor de pa m'obre la gana
i els crits dels fills
m'estiren per les mànigues.
Trobo un bes oblidat
que em puja als llavis.
Somric, i s'obren les finestres.
El sol és tot un altre.

M'agrada molt de veure
els parracs del vestit de soldat
que fan de baieta
i el vell diccionari
que serveix
perquè el petit s'enfili.

Now I'm close to home. A smell of bread makes me feel hungry, and the children's shouts tug at my sleeves. I find a forgotten kiss which rises to my lips. I smile and the windows open. The sun is completely different.

I love to see the tatters of the soldier's uniform used as a floorcloth and the old dictionary that serves for the youngest child to climb on.

Parlem a quatre veus
quan som a taula.

Parlem
de coses virolades
que tot seguit s'esfumen,
o de coses molt netes
que es queden penjades al sostre
per sempre.

Al carrer
m'he deixat,
oblidades,
les paraules de fora.
M'esperen.

XAVIER AMORÓS

We speak with four voices when we're at table.

We talk of many-coloured things that vanish straight away, or of very clean ones that stay hanging from the ceiling for ever.

I have left behind in the street, forgotten, the outdoor words. They are waiting for me.

EL TRULL

A camp ras sota la boira quieta
trobo un trull i penso:
encara tu, cilindre net i força justa.
De mica en mica,
l'ampla boirina assolellada
se'm beu els ulls i m'obre al temps.
En una clariana tèbia
—si en somni breu o llarg, jo no ho sabria
—veig els bous d'un vell novembre d'or.
Quan torno en mi, freda buidor, m'adono
de la fusta plana i seca, taula
de força on dempeus anava l'home,
i fora camp cerco la vila.

SEGIMON SERRALLONGA

The Oilpress

Out in the open under the still mist I find an oilpress and think: you here still, clean cylinder and correct force. Little by little, the wide sunlit haze drinks up my eyes and opens me to time. In a mild clearing—whether in a short or a long dream, I wouldn't know—I see the oxen of an old, golden November. When I come to, a cold emptiness, I notice the flat, dry plank, the platform of force where the man trod at his work, and beyond the fields I seek the town.

EL CAÇADOR

La vinya enveja el verd dels castanyers,
la mar perd son color sota la boira,
s'apaga l'or torrat de la perdiu,
en l'aire hi ha tendreses moridores.
L'estiu se'n va. I un caçador cansat,
amb una breu escopetada,
trenca a bocins el vidre clar del cel
i sobre el món les flors del cel escampa.

TOMÀS GARCÉS

The Hunter

The vineyard envies the green of the chestnut trees, the sea loses its colour under fog, the burnished gold of the partridge is extinguished, in the air there are dying tendernesses. Summer is going away. And a tired hunter, with one brief gunshot, smashes to smithereens the bright glass of the sky and scatters its flowers over the world.

FESTA

Vine al recer d'aquesta cala,
asseu-te a l'ombra dels arbres vinclats
pel seu mateix desig de mar (quines arrels
poden ser tan cruels per retenir-los?).
Vine i no diguis res, que sigui dolç
de veure'ns com objectes vius
d'alentits moviments, que ens donen l'aire
una mica irreal, com somniant-nos, deslliurats
de l'odiosa i persistent tirania del temps.
Deixem parlar la pell—tresor ofert als ulls—
tensada per la força dels paisatges interns
on cada múscul obeeix les ordres
procedents del desig. Després que vinguin
les paraules als llavis, que ens passegin
pel món embolcallat de la memòria,
i aturem-nos als prats dels records més llunyans,
cap als rius clars on ens porti l'atzar. Convida'm

Holiday

Come into the shelter of this cove, sit down in the shade of these trees bent over by their very desire for the sea (what roots could be so cruel as to restrain them?). Come and say nothing, let it be nice to see ourselves as living objects of slowed motions that make us seem slightly unreal, as if dreaming of ourselves, freed from the odious and persistent tyranny of time. Let's let our flesh talk—a treasure offered to the eyes —tensed by the force of interior landscapes where every muscle obeys the orders issued by desire. Let words come later to the lips, let them take us through this world enveloped in memory and let us halt in the meadows of most distant recollections, beside the clear river where fate may carry us. Invite me

a cada estança dels teus anys passats;
entra tu dins els meus, i es mantindrà,
a cada llavi, la llum del somriure,
que fa els rostres més bells (tots els dolors
ja l'han perdut, aquest combat, i ho celebrem
com soldats que reposen de la guerra
festejant i fent festa).

Les mans, sense adonar-nos-en, es troben
i inicien el joc; els ulls s'avenen
a contemplar la dansa de llurs ombres
a la sorra, figures que s'amaguen
darrere els tremolors de l'ombra de les fulles.

SALVADOR OLIVA

to each chamber of your past years and you come into mine, and on each lip
will remain the light of that smile which makes faces more beautiful (all
pains have now lost the fight and we celebrate like soldiers who rest from war
in courtship and merriment).

Our hands, without our realizing it, find each other and begin the game; our
eyes combine to gaze at the dance of their shadows on the sand, shapes
which conceal themselves behind the trembling shadows of the leaves.

SOLSTICI

L'estiu ha bandejat aquest cadàver
ert de la primavera. I ara l'ull
no copsarà les tenebroses ones,
llençol de resplendor lívida. El fenc
es consumeix, talment un llamp que crema,
arbre immolat. Sarments, combats sulfuris
d'arrels, remor terral. De tants guerrers
quarter d'hivern, oh cor de l'home! Estius
i primaveres àvides. L'ardor
febril del temps que el meu passat esquinça
i ens mostra el sol roent i negre. ¿Fórem
nosaltres, guardians d'un joc d'escacs
infaust, de torres i peons la llòbrega
comparsa? Regne del silenci, roures,
tardor de l'ésser. I els metalls, exsangües
sota l'empremta, l'alt domini. Estiu,

Solstice

Summer has exiled the stiff corpse of spring. And now the eye will not catch the dark waves, shroud of livid splendour. The hay is consumed, like a burning lightning-flash, sacrificial tree. Vine shoots, sulphurous conflicts of roots, murmur of earth. Winter quarters of so many warriors, o heart of man! Avid summers and springs. The feverish passion of time which tears up my past and shows us the scorching black sun. Were we, guardians of an ill-fated game of chess, the sombre retinue of castles and pawns? Kingdom of silence, oak-trees, autumn of being. And the metals, bloodless beneath the footprint, the high dominion. Summer,

[83]

estiu sotmès! És una transparència
el cel gelat. El mar, llis, reflecteix
el diamant, la lluna soterrada,
el senyoriu del sol ocult. Els mots
celen un clos pregon, i l'escriptura
lacera el cos del tigre. Escrit amb foc
i escrit amb llum, a la lunar contrada,
pasturatge dels morts. L'amant albira,
enllà dels membres enllaçats, l'obscur.
I les arrels no es mouen. Com els cossos,
s'han nodrit de silenci. Llur país
de sequedat i de centelles obre
els ulls, esbatanats. El crit del corb
sagna al cel moradenc. Fusta i safirs:
l'últim fulgor, convuls, de llum terrestre.

PERE GIMFERRER

submissive summer! The frozen sky is a transparency. The sea, smooth,
reflects the diamond, the buried moon, the mastery of the hidden sun. Words
conceal a deep enclosure, and writing lacerates the body of the tiger. Written
with fire and written with light, in the moon's domain, pasture of the dead.
The lover glimpses darkness beyond the twisting limbs. And the roots do not
move. Like bodies, they have fed on silence. Their land of dryness and sparks
opens its eyes wide. The cry of the raven bleeds in the purple sky. Wood and
sapphires: the last convulsive brilliance of earthly light.

SEXTINA A JOAN MIRO

En el seu vuitanta-cinquè aniversari

El somni toca i mira ple de vida,
i sorgeix l'home d'un conjunt de ratlles;
els braços fan de banyes; a les taques
el sol obre el perfil de tot de signes,
i un nocturn nou, passat a foc i a flames,
esmenta el carnaval d'avui i sempre.

La vida expressa els seus desigs de sempre,
Els elements avancen, donen vida
i resten brasa de les seves flames.
Entre estels lineals de quatre ratlles
les formes es confonen amb els signes,
talment una harmonia emesa amb taques.

Sestina for Joan Miró

on his 85th birthday

The dream touches and gazes full of *life*, and man arises from a set of *lines*; his arms are like horns; in *paint marks* the sun opens the profile of many *signs*, and a new night, passed through fire and *flames*, alludes to the carnaval of today and *always*.

Life expresses its *eternal* desires, the elements advance, give *life* and extract embers from its *flames*. Among linear stars of four *lines* forms are confused with *signs*, like a harmony transmitted with *paint marks*.

(Aquí l'element aigua són les taques.
Espai i aire van units, com sempre.
La terra en aquests quadres són els signes
—més que tenebres, claredat i vida—.
El foc esmola l'ungla de les ratlles
si dels punts de color sorgeixen flames.)

Miró camina intacte entre les flames.
Una arrel regalima i peten taques,
nassos i trompes escarneixen ratlles,
i els ulls miren els ulls, miralls de sempre.
Voltat de galls, Miró pinta la vida
i viu els quadres, hortolà de signes.

The dream touches and gazes full of *life*, and man arises (Here the element of water is the *paint marks*. Space and air are united, as *always*. The earth in these pictures is *signs*—more than darkness, clarity and life— Fire hones the finger-nail of the *lines* if *flames* arise from the points of colour.)

Miró walks unharmed among the *flames*. A root streams with liquid and *paint marks* explode, noses and trunks mock at *lines*, and eyes gaze at eyes, *eternal* mirrors. Surrounded by roosters, Miró paints *life* and lives his pictures, gardener of *signs*.

La llum i el so, els percebem als signes.
La llibertat és vista i emet flames.
Puja pels peus la força de la vida;
canta i més canta el blau d'un fons de taques
i broten fulles del cos humà, sempre
enllà del pensament teixit a ratlles.

Deixem el sol a terra sense ratlles.
La lluna ve de lluny i parla amb signes,
però els seus raigs no es perden perquè sempre
s'acosten a l'origen quatre flames
amb cresta o barretina. Així les taques
no ens priven que tornem de mort a vida.

Miró dóna la vida amb punts i ratlles;
l'alè surt de les taques i dels signes,
i amor i flames restaran per sempre.

JOAN BROSSA

Light and sound, we perceive them in the *signs*. Liberty is seen and gives off *flames*. The power of *life* mounts through the feet; the blue of a background of *paint marks* sings and sings and leaves spring from the human body, *always* beyond thought woven in *lines*.

We leave the sun on the ground without *lines*. The moon comes from a long way off and speaks in *signs*, but its rays are not lost since *always* four *flames* with a cock's crest or a *barretina* approach the origin. Thus the *paint-marks* do not prevent us from returning from death to *life*.

Miró gives *life* with dots and *lines*: breath comes out of the *paint marks* and the *signs*, and love and *flames* will remain *for ever*.

Ni tots els ulls alhora que Picasso
pintà als autoretrats inquisitius,
ni tots els ulls de Goethe en els millors
retrats que li pintaren,

no saben descobrir-me en el mirall,
no poden inventar-me cap destí,
no volen aclarir-me cap camí
i lentament s'apaguen.

Envejo nens petits amb uns grans ulls
que tot ho descobreixen, vivacíssims,
que juguen amb el món amb tanta eufòria,
que tot ho posseeixen.

I, trist, trec els meus ulls a passejar
per places i carrers, com els veïns
passegen cada vespre el seu gosset,
abans que tot s'acabi.

DAVID JOU

Not even all those eyes, staring as one from the searching self-portraits painted by Picasso, nor all of Goethe's eyes looking on from the best portraits painted of him,

can catch sight of me in the mirror, invent a fate for me, nor can they shed light on any path I might take, and slowly they grow dim.

I envy those small children with wide-open eyes, so sharp to catch everything, who play so rapturously with the world, and own it all.

So, sadly, I take my eyes out for a stroll through squares and streets, like my neighbours who walk their puppy each evening, before it all comes to an end.

PASSING-SHOT

Instal·lat ja de temps en una
plataforma de somnis
estèrils, desfibrats, sense un ordit,
per contrast amb el joc
de cada dia a la pista
vermella, piconada,
on reboten duríssimes a cada
cop les pilotes de fúria que em llancen
els contraris,
    com un boig, ara al fons,
ara a la xarxa, intento córrer,
saltar, ajupir-me, redreçar-me,
mai prou flexible, mai prou fort, mai a temps
a tornar els *passing-shots* que em tiren
a cada instant.

Passing Shot

Well installed on a raised stand of sterile dreams that are frayed and patternless in contrast to the daily game on the rolled red court where, at each stroke, the furious balls that my adversaries unleash bounce sharply, I like a mad thing, now at the base-line, now at the net, try to run, to drive, to bend, to stretch up, never flexible enough, never strong enough, never in time to return the passing shots that come at me every second.

Sé prou que tinc
perduda la partida, que de res
no serveixen els breus
moments de descans entre joc
i joc, la tovallola humida
que et mulla el front, el vas
de tònica o de te
            —no cal pensar en el dòping,
que per això ja és tard.
      Ara jo dic: què fer
de la resta de vida que em queda,
massa gastada, massa inútil
per seguir el joc?
      M'ho sé: fins a l'últim
dia de tots
aniré mal corrent, mal caient, no sabent
o no tenint valor per acabar
sense un crit ni una queixa.

M'instal·lo novament
a la petita plataforma
dels somnis, cada cop
més fràgil, sempre a punt
de caure i despertar-me
del tot.
                        JOAN VINYOLI

I know full well that I have lost the match, that I shall gain nothing from the brief moments of respite between games, from the damp towel to dab the brow, the glass of tonic water or tea—there is no point in thinking about drugs, it is too late for that now. So now I say: what is to be done with the rest of my life, too worn out, too useless to keep playing? I know: right until the very last I'll go stumbling and blundering through, not knowing how, or not being brave enough, to call it a day without protest or complaint.,

Up I go again on to my little platform of dreams, more and more fragile, always on the verge of collapse and of waking up completely.

[90]

Si gravita al meu cor la lluna de les illes
m'ofego en l'atmosfera d'un delta nebulós
i el clima de les flautes dilata lentament
un nucli de solubles planetes boreals.

La tempesta a la jungla agita les palmeres.
Javelines indígenes dobleguen els jaguars.
El meu somni governa canoes i piragües.
Desemboquen en mi afluents navegables.

Em divideix el cor la quilla dels vaixells
carregats de productes—cotons, laques, espècies—
que tripula el destí vers la ignota metròpoli
de l'angoixa i la freda tenebra ultramarina.

El vent cruix a les veles de lones impol·lutes
i vibren tots els cables i els màstils dels navilis
mentre s'entela el cel, polint blaus esmerils
i una líquida làmina d'aluminis translúcids.

JOAN M. PUIGVERT

If the moon of the islands is drawn to my heart, I drown in the atmosphere of
a nebulous delta and the climate of flutes slowly dilates a nucleus of soluble,
boreal planets.

The storm in the jungle shakes the palm trees. Native javelins tame the
jaguars. My dream masters canoes and piraguas. Navigable tributaries flow
into me.

My heart is divided by the keels of vessels loaded with produce—cottons,
lacquers, spices—which destiny crews towards the unknown metropolis of
anguish and of cold darkness beyond the seas.

The wind creaks in the sails of spotless canvas and all the ships' cables and
masts vibrate, as the sky clouds over, buffing blue emeries and a liquid sheet
of translucent aluminiums.

[91]

LA FI DEL MÓN

La fi del món començarà un estiu,
just quan arribin les primeres noies
de pits menuts i cuixes llargues
i els primers nois d'ulls blaus,
rossos i hermafrodites.

En Biel Ferrater serà una papallona
i volarà, finalment alliberat,
ran de les sines joves.

Començarà un estiu la fi del món,
sense aldarulls profètics ni trompetes,
indolentment, com si fos un assaig
de fi del món i no la fi mateixa.

The End of the World

The end of the world will begin one summer, just on the arrival of the first girls with tiny breasts and long thighs and the first boys, blue-eyed, blond and hermaphrodite.

Biel Ferrater will be a butterfly and will flutter, finally freed, around the young breasts.

One summer the end of the world will begin, without prophetic tumult or trumpets, lazily, as if it were a rehearsal for the end of the world and not the end itself.

Hi haurà gent a les platges, i crepuscles,
i amors novells, i paraules mig dites,
i adulteris tendríssims, i esperances,
i vent i sol i pluja.

Hi haurà el mateix de qualsevol estiu:
neguits, amors, misteris, solituds,
i cap ocell no deturarà el vol,
cap fosc auguri no farà estremir
les parelles que es besin
per primera vegada.
Tot serà plàcid, vehement i clar,
discretament solemne tal vegada,
i si esclaten senyals de desmesura
serà en indrets exòtics

o bé entre gent que sempre ocupa llocs
destacats a les cròniques.

There'll be people on the beaches and sunsets and first loves and half-spoken words and the tenderest of adulteries and hopes and wind and sun and rain.

There'll be the same things as any other summer: anxieties, loves, mysteries, solitudes and no bird will halt its flight, no dark omen will cause the couples who kiss for the first time to tremble. All will be placid, vehement and bright, discreetly solemn, perhaps, and if any signs of immoderation crop up it will be in exotic places

or else among people who figure prominently in the gossip columns.

Només potser un poeta,
primicer, però ja notablement marrit,
un vespre inesperat sentirà que un calfred
li solca l'espinada
i absurdament tancarà la finestra
desoint la gran crida
per la grotesca por d'un corrent d'aire.

Durarà tot l'estiu la fi del món,
sense perdre un instant aquell punt agredolç
d'indolència i joc del principi,
i al capdavall, un dia qualsevol
de finals de setembre,
el sol s'enfonsarà lentament dins el mar
en un crepuscle esplendorós i tràgic.

I tot serà silenci ja per sempre.

MIQUEL MARTÍ I POL

A single poet, perhaps, first-rate but already noticeably depressed, will feel, one unexpected evening, a shiver furrowing his spine and, absurdly, will close the window, not hearing the great cry through his grotesque fear of a draught.

The end of the world will last all summer, without losing for a moment that bittersweet point of indolence and play of the beginning and, finally, one day towards the end of September, the sun will sink slowly in the sea in a splendid and tragic twilight.

And everything will be silence then for ever.

POEMS INCLUDED IN THE ANTHOLOGY

FELIU FORMOSA (b. 1934) 'Tot allò que diem. . .'

FRANCESC VALLVERDÚ (b. 1935) *Sonet a Ausiàs March*

ROSA LEVERONI (1910-85) *Cinc poemes desolats*

AGUSTÍ BARTRA (1908-82) 'Quan de mi, finalment. . .'

MARTA PESSARRODONA (b. 1941) *In memoriam*

NARCÍS COMADIRA (b. 1942) *Primavera anglesa*

MARIÀ MANENT (b. 1898) *El David de la Catedral de Salisbury*

JOAN MARGARIT (b. 1938) *Instantània*

ÀLEX SUSANNA (b. 1957) *Cases amb grans arbres*

XAVIER AMORÓS (b. 1923) 'Ara sóc a la falda de casa. . .'

SEGIMON SERRALLONGA (b. 1930) *El trull*

TOMÀS GARCÉS (b. 1901) *El caçador*

SALVADOR OLIVA (b. 1942) *Festa*

PERE GIMFERRER (b. 1945) *Solstici*

JOAN BROSSA (b. 1919) *Sextina a Joan Miró*

DAVID JOU (b. 1953) 'Ni tots els ulls. . .'

JOAN VINYOLI (1914-84) *Passing-shot*

JOAN M. PUIGVERT (b. 1959) 'Si gravita al meu cor la lluna de les illes. . .'

MIQUEL MARTÍ I POL (b. 1929) *La fi del món*

TABULA GRATULATORIA

Christopher Amies

Ma. Antònia Babí i Vila

David Barrass

Tine Barrass

Joaquim Bartrons i Casas

Amanda Bath

Concepció Batista i Roca

Júlia Bordas de Hall

Max Cahner

Richard A. Cardwell

G.J.G. Cheyne

Carme Claret

Rosa Coll-Andreu

Josep Duran Rubiralta

M.F. Escurriola i Gràcia

Joaquim Espinosa i Pedrola

Henry Ettinghausen

Desmond Gailey

David George

Salvador Giner

John Gornall

Helen F. Grant

Alexander Grigg

Keith Hall

Frank Llewelyn Harrison

Albert Hauf

Úrsula Hauf

Rita J. Humble

Helen Hughes-Brock

Jacqueline Hurtley

Antoni Ibarz

Margaret Johnson

Ron Keightley

Dominic Keown

Lord Kilmarnock

Tess Knighton

Patricia Langdon-Davies

R.H. Langdon-Davies

Josep G. Llauradó

Derek W. Lomax

Marilyn McCully

David Mackay

M.R. Martin

Lourdes Melcion

Francesc de B. Moll

Josep M. Moretó

R. Perera

Frank Pierce

Montserrat Pla

Stuart C. Poole

Robert Pring-Mill

Michael Raeburn

Oriol Ramis-Juan

Carme Rius de Menezes

Mercè Roca Hospital

Josep Roca-Pons

Eamonn Rodgers
J.M. Ruiz Veintemilla
Paul Russell-Gebbett
Peter Rycraft
Rafael Sala
D. de G. Sells
Amadeu Solé-Leris
Tilbert Dídac Stegmann
Julia Strevens
Michael Strubell
R.B. Tate
Amèlia Trueta
Antoni Turull
Pamela Waley
Anna Walker
Geoffrey Walker
Max W. Wheeler
Judith Willis
Alison Wright
Alan Yates